C000292516

Merrythought
Bears

Dedication

For Alastair and Amy with love and gratitude.

Merrythought Bears

Kathy Martin

First published in Great Britain in 2009 by
REMEMBER WHEN
An imprint of
Pen & Sword Books Ltd
47 Church Street
Barnsley
South Yorkshire
S70 2AS

Copyright © Kathy Martin 2009

ISBN 978 1 84468 032 0

The right of Kathy Martin to be identified as Author of this work has
been asserted by her in accordance with the Copyright, Designs and
Patents Act 1988.

A CIP catalogue record for this book is available from the British
Library.

All rights reserved. No part of this book may be reproduced or trans-
mitted in any form or by any means, electronic or mechanical
including photocopying, recording or by any information storage and
retrieval system, without permission from the Publisher in writing.

Typeset by Phoenix Typesetting, Auldgirth, Dumfriesshire
Printed and bound by Kyodo Nation Printing Services Co., Ltd

Pen & Sword Books Ltd incorporates the imprints of Pen & Sword
Aviation, Pen & Sword Maritime, Pen & Sword Military, Wharncliffe
Local History, Pen & Sword Select, Pen & Sword Military Classics,
Leo Cooper, Remember When, Seaforth Publishing and Frontline
Publishing.

For a complete list of Pen & Sword titles please contact
PEN & SWORD BOOKS LIMITED
47 Church Street, Barnsley, South Yorkshire, S70 2AS, England
E-mail: enquiries@pen-and-sword.co.uk
Website: www.pen-and-sword.co.uk

Contents

Teddy Bear Time Line

The key events of teddy bear history are listed below while significant Merrythought events are indicated by a ☛.

1902
- German company Margarete Steiff GmbH, creates first ever teddy bear (although the name 'teddy' is not yet used)
- US President Theodore Roosevelt becomes associated with the new bear toy after refusing to shoot a captive bear during a hunting trip on the Louisiana/Mississippi border
- Shopkeepers Morris and Rose Michtom of Brooklyn, New York, create their own stuffed toy bear following Roosevelt's well-publicised refusal to shoot the captive bear; demand skyrockets and Ideal Novelty and Toy Co. is born

1904
- Roosevelt adopts the teddy bear as his mascot during his successful campaign for re-election

1905
- Steiff produce the first disc-jointed teddy bear (string and rods had previously been used); the disc method, which uses two card circles connected by a cotter pin, is still widely used today

1906
- *Playthings*, an American toy trade publication, coins the term 'teddy bear' for the first time (as opposed to the previously used 'Teddy's bear', Teddy being Theodore Roosevelt)
- Canadian-born writer Seymour Eaton publishes *The Roosevelt Bears: Their Travels and Adventures*, first in a wildly popular series of books about teddies
- Harrods advertises Steiff's 'soft jointed bear' in its catalogue

1907
- High demand sees the Steiff factory produce just under one million teddy bears
- William Gordon Holmes and George H. Laxton join forces to found a worsted spinning firm in Oakworth, West Yorkshire

1908
- J.K. Farnell produce the first British teddy bear
- Dean's Rag Book Co. makes a cut-out-and-sew printed cloth teddy

1910
- Harrods start selling bears made by J.K. Farnell

1914
- Outbreak of First World War sees UK ban on all German imports, including teddy bears

1915
- British toy firms, including Chad Valley and Dean's Rag Book, begin to manufacture mohair teddy bears

1920
- Mary Tourtel creates Rupert Bear for the *Daily Express*

1921
- Daphne Milne, wife of playwright Alan Alexander Milne, buys a teddy from Harrods for the first birthday of her son, Christopher Robin; the bear is soon to be immortalised as Winnie the Pooh

1924
- Pooh makes a brief, unnamed appearance in *When We Were Very Young*, a volume of children's verse by A.A. Milne

1926
- A.A. Milne's *Winnie-the-Pooh* is published by Methuen & Co., with illustrations by E.H. Shepard

1929
- Manufacturers start to make teddies from artificial silk plush

1930
- ☞ Merrythought is founded by William Gordon Holmes and George H. Laxton; Clifton Rendle and Henry Janisch run the company: Florence Attwood designs the bears
- ☞ First Merrythought catalogue is produced, introducing Bingie, Tumpy, the Merrythought and the Magnet Bear

1933
- • Lyricist Jimmy Kennedy writes words to 'Teddy Bears' Picnic', a tune composed in 1907 by John Bratton
- ☞ Merrythought introduces dressed Bingies

1937
- ☞ Pandas debut in Merrythought range

1938
- • Chad Valley receives Royal Warrant from Queen Elizabeth, wife of George VI and mother of Princess Elizabeth, later Queen Elizabeth II

1939
- • Second World War begins, temporarily halting virtually all production of British teddy bears

1946
- ☞ Merrythought return to Ironbridge premises and production restarts

1948
- • Screw-in safety eyes patented by Wendy Boston

1949
- ☞ Trayton Holmes, son of William Gordon, joins Merrythought after death of Managing Director, Clifton Rendle
- ☞ Florence Attwood leaves Merrythought due to ill health
- ☞ Merrythought create Punkinhead toy for Eaton's in Canada

1952
- • Harry Corbett's Sooty makes TV debut and Chad Valley secure Sooty merchandising rights
- ☞ Dean's Managing Director, Jimmy Matthews, starts to represent Merrythought
- ☞ Jean Barber joins Merrythought as replacement for Florence Attwood

1955

- First fully washable teddy bear demonstrated on TV by Wendy Boston company

1956

- BBC cameraman Michael Bond buys a lonely teddy bear from Selfridges department store
- ☛ Ursula Moray Williams' 'Woppit', a bear character from the *Robin* comic, is produced by Merrythought

1957

- ☛ Merrythought's Cheeky Bear, designed by Jean Barber, goes on sale

1958

- Michael Bond's *A Bear Called Paddington* is published by William Collins

1959

- New safety eye with nylon screw introduced by Wendy Boston

1965

- ☛ Twisty toys including Mr & Mrs Twisty Bear introduced by Merrythought

1966

- Disney release *Winnie the Pooh and the Honey-Tree*
- ☛ Merrythought produce first Winnie the Pooh toy
- ☛ Jean Barber leaves Merrythought

1967

- ☛ Donald Campbell dies attempting new water speed record on Coniston Water; his mascot, Mr Whoppit (Merrythought's Woppit), is recovered

1969

- Publication of actor Peter Bull's *Bear With Me* awakes interest in collecting teddy bears

1972

- ☛ Jacqueline Revitt and Oliver Holmes join Merrythought

1979

- Marquis of Bath hosts teddy bear rally at Longleat, his country seat

1981

- Granada TV's adaptation of Evelyn Waugh's *Brideshead Revisited* brings fame to Delicatessen, an old bear belonging to Peter Bull which is cast in the role of Aloysius

1985

- Ian Pout opens Teddy Bears of Witney, the first shop in the UK to specialise in selling old and new teddy bears

1988

- Gyles Brandreth opens The Teddy Bear Museum in Stratford-upon-Avon

1989

- Alfonzo, a rare red Steiff bear which once belonged to Princess Xenia of Russia, is sold at Christie's for £12,100; bought by Ian Pout, he becomes the figurehead of Teddy Bears of Witney
- Happy, a 1926 Steiff bear made from dual plush mohair, makes a world record price at Sotheby's of £55,000

1990

- ☞ Merrythought celebrate their 60th anniversary with a limited edition Diamond Jubilee Bear

1992

- Steiff launch a worldwide collectors' club
- ☞ Jacqueline Revitt's Master Mischief wins a TOBY and Golden Teddy Award

1993

- Christie's South Kensington holds first auction dedicated solely to teddy bears

1994

- Teddy Girl, a 1904 cinnamon Steiff bear with impeccable provenance, sells at Christie's South Kensington for a new world record price of £110,000

1995
- Launch of Merrythought International Collectors' Club

1996
- First Open Day for Merrythought International Collectors' Club members

1998
- Opening of Puppenhausmuseum in Basel, Switzerland, where visitors can see over 2,000 teddies dating mostly before 1950

2000
- At a charity auction in Monaco, a new world record for teddies is set when a modern Steiff bear (dressed by Louis Vuitton) sells for £130,000

2001
- Merrythought's Hope Bear raises money for the World Trade Center Disaster Fund

2002
- Centenary of the teddy bear is marked by a flurry of commemorative bears and a special auction at Christie's South Kensington

2005
- Jacqueline Revitt is made redundant from Merrythought

2006
- Directors announce closure of Merrythought Toys Ltd. through voluntary liquidation

2007
- Last teddy bear auction held at Christie's South Kensington
- Assets, work in progress and stock of Merrythought Toys Ltd. is bought by its holding company, Merrythought Ltd.
- Merrythought is relaunched in small section of the original Ironbridge factory

Foreword

IWAS BORN in Germany. I am not German. My parents were stationed in Germany after the Second World War and I was born in a British Forces Hospital in Wuppertal. When we returned from Germany to Great Britain in the early 1950s, apart from me, we brought back only two precious items that could be said to be 'made in Germany' – our car and my teddy bear.

Today I like to think that, if asked to name their all-time favourite German invention, most British people would put the teddy bear second only to the automobile – and, perhaps, in these environmentally-aware times the sensible ones would put the teddy bear first.

The world's favourite soft toy first appeared in Britain in 1905 and swiftly captured the public's affections, no small accomplishment for a German toy named after an American President. Within a few years of its arrival in Great Britain, the teddy bear had become the nation's most popular toy and its image was used to sell everything from china plates to picture postcards.

In the early years of the Twentieth Century the majority of teddy bears occupying place of honour in our grandparents' nurseries were of German manufacture, since few British toy companies – J.K. Farnell being one notable exception – rose to the challenge of making the new toy. It took a ban on German imports during the First World War to change that, but once production was under way firms such as Dean's Rag Book, Chad Valley and Harwin & Co. joined Farnell and others in keeping British children supplied with teddy bears. In time these impressive pioneers were joined by other great manufacturers, including Merrythought, but sadly, during the last decades of the Twentieth Century, all but a handful disappeared. Today, just Merrythought remains, creating teddy bears from the same small town in which it was founded in 1930, and run by the grandson of one of the founders.

More than any other British soft toy manufacturer, Merrythought has cast a spell over generations of teddy-bear lovers, children and adults alike. Longevity and continuity are part of the reason the company is so well-loved but there is much more to it than that. A passionate arctophile herself, Kathy Martin has delved into the history of the company, searching for an explanation as to why Merrythought has survived when so many others have fallen. Along the way she has unearthed much fascinating and hitherto forgotten information about the origins of the company, its products and the people who made it all happen. I love teddy bears. If you love teddy bears too, you are going to love this book.

Gyles Brandreth

Founder of The Teddy Bear Museum,
now housed at the Polka Children's Theatre in Wimbledon,
London, SW19 1SB

Did you know . . . that 'arctophile' is the word used to describe a teddy bear enthusiast?

Introduction

⋙►◈◄⋘

O N NOVEMBER 27th, 2006, Merrythought Toys Ltd. announced that it was going into voluntary liquidation. Officially, the closure of this much-loved teddy bear and soft toy producer was blamed on fierce competition from foreign imports, although in an article written by Edward Heathcoat Amory for *The Daily Mail* newspaper, Managing Director Oliver Holmes also pointed an accusing finger at government legislation and high taxes.

News of the company's demise brought bitter disappointment to Merrythought's dedicated collectors. Within hours of word getting out, members of the Merrythought International Collectors' Club were bombarding the club's website with requests for clarification of the situation. As Editor, at the time, of the UK's leading teddy bear magazine, I also received many letters and emails from Merrythought fans, all expressing disbelief and a sense of overwhelming loss. One wrote that she had been 'completely devastated' to learn of the company's closure, and others simply stated that losing Merrythought felt like losing a close family friend. 'I suppose I took it for granted, believing it would always be there,' one distraught collector told me soon after the closure, 'and now I can't believe it's gone. I don't think I'll ever take anything for granted again.'

Ironically, if inevitably, once the factory gates had closed for what everyone believed to be the final time, demand for Merrythought products leapt to levels unseen for many years. Shop stock that had been gathering dust on shelves for months was suddenly snapped up by collectors anxious for their last Merrythought fix, while on eBay prices rocketed for Merrythought items old and new. For a few weeks, virtually anything with a Merrythought label was guaranteed to sell well, although as one well known teddy bear expert pointed out at the time, 'There's no reason for the price of old Merrythoughts to go up. Just because the factory has closed now, there's still going to be the same number of vintage Merrythoughts as there was before the closure.'

In fact, as the public was about to discover, reports of Merrythought's death were greatly exaggerated (to paraphrase the famous Mark Twain quotation). Virtually within days of the company's closure, rumours started circulating that it was soon going to rise, phoenix-style, from the ashes. Nobody would comment officially but by December 2006, several major retailers had told me (off the record) that they knew there would be new Merrythought products available for sale in 2007. Sure enough, by the spring of 2007, Merrythought was producing toys once again, albeit in a vastly reduced capacity. Just a fraction of the original workforce was rehired and set to work in a small section of the Ironbridge factory.

A statement, put out by Oliver Holmes at the time of the company's relaunch, suggested that the support he had received from the public played a part in the revival of Merrythought:

> *It is with both a sense of relief and pride that we present to you the* Merrythought *2007 catalogue. November 2006 saw the much lamented demise of* Merrythought Toys Ltd *and almost the end for the great British Teddy Bear. Who, after all, can boast hand-made British bears that have enjoyed continued production for over three quarters of a century?*
>
> *The huge media outcry and public support following our announced closure caused countrywide pandemonium as collectors hurriedly cleared shelves of every piece of available* Merrythought, *worried that it could be their last opportunity to buy one of our bears. This huge show of support and tremendous following for our products has prompted staff here to appraise the possibility of a much condensed 2007 collection. The tough market conditions that spelled the end for* Merrythought Toys Ltd *has resulted in a much sharper, collector-focused group of products that is able to pride itself on using the finest quality materials and the best of British manufacture, here in a small section of the original factory site in Ironbridge, Shropshire. We hope you will enjoy our new range and continue to support* Merrythought *– still creating Britain's best loved bears.*

While the company's closure had merited many column inches in the daily newspapers, news of its rebirth went largely unnoticed by the press. It was a different story, though, for collectors and those generally interested in teddy bears; for them the news was precisely what they had been hoping to hear. Even though most were realistic enough to understand that things would never be exactly the same, they nevertheless felt immense relief that Merrythought had been salvaged in some form at least. This poses the question, why should people care so much about the wavering fortunes of a Shropshire toy factory?

The answer lies in the past. Merrythought was by no means the first British toy company to create teddy bears. In fact, it arrived on the scene rather late, appearing in 1930, some twenty-two years after J.K. Farnell produced the first British teddy. But the company more than made up for its tardy start by creating some of the most memorable designs of the ensuing decades. From the earliest bears such as the Bingie Sitting Cub, which appeared in the firm's very first catalogue, to later designs like the iconic, best-selling Cheeky Bear, Merrythought made a massive impact on the soft toy market. That impact was felt not just at home in Britain but right around the world; in its heyday the company had an international reputation for excellence, and even today the Merrythought name elicits a positive response in Japan, the USA, Canada, Australia and many other far-flung nations. Merrythought holds a special place in the public's affection, but while it may be no surprise that arctophiles (people passionate about bears) revere the brand, it is quite remarkable that many individuals with no special interest in teddy bears not only know the

Bingie debuted in
Merrythought's very
first catalogue.

The iconic Cheeky Bear has been a firm favourite since its introduction in 1957.

Merrythought name, but also recognise it as synonymous with quality and an indefinable British-ness. When speaking to members of the public about my work as a teddy bear writer, I have frequently found they are familiar with the names of just two teddy manufacturers: Steiff (the German firm that invented the teddy bear) and Merrythought. Perhaps surprisingly, very few know the name of the company that made their own childhood teddy bear but almost everyone has heard of Merrythought.

This fame is quite remarkable considering that Merrythought is, after all, a relatively small company but I believe one reason for it lies in the firm's longevity. Merrythought has survived where other, older soft toys firms have not. Close rival J.K. Farnell ceased trading in the 1960s, while Chad Valley, another competitor, clung on for a further decade before disappearing (although the brand name was later acquired by Woolworths). They were the lucky ones, as many other British teddy manufacturers folded prior to this; victims of cheaper imported bears and a temporary loss of interest in traditional soft toys. Only one British teddy bear manufacturer that was around when Merrythought began trading in 1930 remains in existence today, and that is Dean's, which made its first teddy bear in 1915. Therefore, if any British teddy manufacturer deserves pre-eminence, a case could be made for Dean's, were it not for two major differences between Dean's and Merrythought. The first is that ownership of Dean's has changed several times, as has its location, whilst Merrythought is a third generation family business operating out of the same Shropshire premises from which it was launched (apart from a brief and unavoidable hiatus during the Second World War). This sense of continuity is another reason why people love Merrythought. The company hasn't just survived, it has survived with its identity intact. If one of the founders were to somehow come back to life and step inside the premises, they would of course find changes but they would recognise the same picturesque location next to Abraham Darby's historic Iron Bridge, and they would note with satisfaction that the company was being run by Oliver Holmes, grandson of one of the cofounders. More than anything, though, they would be pleased to discover that Merrythought bears and toys are still being made in England, in contrast with Dean's bears which are now reportedly manufactured somewhere in the Far East. Longevity, continuity and a tenacious commitment to high quality, domestically made products – this, essentially, is what makes Merrythought so special.

Since falling under Merrythought's spell many years ago, I have always wanted to find out more about its history. Naturally I was aware of certain basic facts that have appeared in numerous publications over the years, but for me they always left unanswered many questions about the 'who, what,

Merrythought bears are still being made in Ironbridge today, nearly eighty years after this bear was made there.

why, where and when' of Merrythought's origins. So I started doing some research of my own, and soon discovered that a lot of the facts that have been taken for granted for years are wholly inaccurate, while others tell only a fraction of the story. Spurred on by my discoveries, I continued digging into old records and generally making a nuisance of myself by asking people endless questions. My research has resulted in a book that offers a wealth of new information concerning Merrythought, its people and its products; a biography of the company as much as a record of the most memorable bears it made. I believe this book will prove equally fascinating to collectors, those that grew up with a Merrythought bear and indeed anyone with more than a passing interest in teddy bears.

In the interests of readability, I have not listed every single teddy bear variation made by the company over its 78-year history but I have endeavoured to mention all the significant designs – a real boon for would-be collectors – as well as a good number of the minor ones. Also for collectors, there is a section with advice on identifying, dating, purchasing and caring for Merrythought teddy bears, and since there was much more to Merrythought than just the teddies, I have included a chapter that looks at their wonderful soft toys. Since this is the first book about the company following its dramatic closure and subsequent resurrection, it also provides an unbiased overview of those events. More than all this, however, I believe the book explains why the continued survival of this intrinsically British company is good news for all teddy bear lovers.

CHAPTER ONE

Origins

Founding fathers: Holmes and Laxton

EARLY IN THE Twentieth Century, a business partnership was formed by two Yorkshire men, William Gordon Holmes (generally known as Gordon) and George H. Laxton. Their business, a worsted spinning firm called Holmes, Laxton & Co., was based at Vale Mills, Oakworth. Oakworth is a Pennine village in the heart of Brontë country, about four miles from Keighley in West Yorkshire. Previous studies of Merrythought have traced the origins of the Holmes/Laxton partnership back to 1919 but there is strong evidence to support an earlier date. Stored in the archives at Bradford Industrial Museum are records about Holmes, Laxton & Co. (relating to the warping book and inventory of Vale Mills) which cover the period 1914 to 1960, proving irrefutably that the partnership began at least five years earlier than is commonly supposed. Furthermore, an even earlier date of 1907 is given by Laxtons, a Yorkshire-based company producing high quality yarns for upholstery and clothing, which is run today by the great-grandson of George H. Laxton. Having celebrated its centenary in 2007, Laxtons published an article about the company's history on its website, in which 1907 is given as the year that George H. Laxton and Gordon Holmes formed their worsted spinning firm. This date is further supported by a brief history of the Holmes family, compiled by family members for their personal interest, in which 1907 is given as the year Gordon Holmes teamed up with George Laxton. Given these facts, it is safe to assume that Holmes and Laxton were in business together a fair bit earlier than has previously been believed.

A few years here or there may seem unimportant, except that by establishing its origins prior to 1914, a compelling explanation for the firm's success becomes apparent. That reason was the advent of the First World War (1914 to 1918). During the war years, the Yorkshire wool industry was stretched to capacity making uniforms for soldiers at the Front. Put bluntly, business would have been booming while the war was raging across Europe, but by

William Gordon Holmes in First World War uniform.

1919 demand was waning. (There was nothing improper in Holmes and Laxton doing well during the war years, quite the contrary in fact, since by providing wool cloth for the nation they were performing a vital function. Furthermore, Gordon Holmes played an active role in the war, enlisting in 1915 and seeing action at the Battle of Cambrai, the first encounter in which tanks played a pivotal role. I have been unable to discover if Laxton fought in the war but given his age – he was 37 at the start of the war – and the importance of his occupation, I feel the likelihood is that he did not).

The new partners brought different skills to the enterprise – Laxton provided the technical expertise while Holmes had the financial acumen. George Laxton was older than Gordon Holmes by eight years but this seniority was not reflected in the name of the business, with Holmes preceding Laxton. Ordinarily in business partnerships an age difference of eight years would not seem great but, assuming the 1907 start date to be correct, Laxton at the time would have been 30 years old while Holmes was just 22. He was doubtless very astute for his age but even so, Laxton's age and experience could have led him to expect first billing in the company's name. Of course, it might be that the decision was made purely for alphabetical reasons or on the toss of a coin, but it seems probable that Gordon Holmes provided the greater part of the start-up capital and therefore wanted his name to come first. Coming from a relatively prosperous family with interests in brewing and farming, he would have found it easier to raise the necessary capital than George Laxton, son of a retired policeman, who worked as manager of a spinning business before the inauguration of Holmes, Laxton & Co.

Laxtons' staff photo taken in the late 1940s; George H. Laxton is seated directly behind the white table, and Gordon Holmes, wearing an overall over his suit, sits four to his left at the end of the row.

From wool to toys: Clifton Rendle and Henry Janisch

During the early years of Holmes, Laxton & Co., the company created and sold worsted, a firmly twisted wool yarn. Then, a little before the outbreak of the First World War, they started to create yarn from imported mohair, using a technology they had developed with local weavers. Business was good for a time, with the war creating an insatiable demand for Yorkshire wool, but with the 1920s came a decline in the market for mohair cloth. This affected Holmes, Laxton & Co. because the weavers to whom they sold their yarn were struggling to find enough business to keep them afloat. One of these customers in particular, a Huddersfield plush weaving business called Dyson Hall & Co., was experiencing great difficulty, so Holmes and Laxton stepped in. They took the somewhat radical step of buying Dyson Hall and then set about finding a new market for the firm's woven mohair.

By lucky chance, the sales director at Dyson Hall was acquainted with a certain Clifton James Rendle, a 39-year-old First World War veteran who managed the Chad Valley Wrekin Toy Works in Wellington, Shropshire. It can have escaped no one's notice that many Chad Valley toys were made from mohair, a material Holmes and Laxton had in abundance. Clearly, here was an opportunity to manufacture something that had an established market.

Rendle had taken up his position with Chad Valley in Wellington around 1925, having previously worked for the same firm's Birmingham factory. For reasons unknown, Rendle now felt ready to move on so when he was approached by Holmes and Laxton to head up their new toy-making venture, he agreed.

When Clifton Rendle left Chad Valley to set up Merrythought, several experienced workers chose to move with him. This says something about him both as a man and a manager, because in those days it required a leap of faith to voluntarily leave secure employment with an established company in order to join a start-up operation. Those who accompanied him when he moved to Merrythought clearly trusted his judgement, and must have enjoyed working with him sufficiently to justify taking the risk.

Since Rendle played a pivotal role in the company's early years, it is worth taking a closer look at him. Although there is not an abundance of information available, there is enough to piece together a sketchy portrait of his personality and abilities. He was born in Fulham in 1891 and his parents – father Frederick, a signwriter, and mother Emily – had three other children. As a skilled tradesman, his father's position in class-conscious, late Nineteenth-Century society would have been somewhere between genteel working class and aspirational lower middle class. This view is borne out by the occupations listed for the Rendles' nearest neighbours in the census of 1901: there are clerks working variously for solicitors, shipbrokers and general commercial organisations; a manageress of a coffee house; a ship's steward; and a china shop assistant. All these occupations, including signwriting, required at least a veneer of refinement as well as the ability to read, write and do basic arithmetic. Thus Rendle's background may have been humble but he would have been equipped with the skills needed to advance in society.

In November 1914, at the age of 23, Clifton Rendle went to France as a private in the North Somerset Yeomanry where he saw action in some of the bloodiest battles ever fought by British troops. In December 1916 he was plucked from the ranks to become a junior officer, joining the Rifle Brigade as a second lieutenant. Such promotions were unusual but not unheard of; at the time, young officers were being slain in such vast numbers that it was necessary to find suitable replacements amongst the other ranks. His superiors clearly thought he was officer material and believed he could lead men in highly challenging circumstances. A further promotion, in June 1918, to the rank of first lieutenant, demonstrates that their confidence in him had not been misplaced.

Although it is unclear what his occupation was prior to 1914, Rendle was living in Weston-Super-Mare when he enlisted. It is possible that during this time he met and was employed by another Weston resident, Henry Swinburne Johnson, one of the Johnson brothers running Chad Valley. Speculation aside, what is known for certain is that in 1917, one year before the war ended, Rendle married Elsie Beatrice Chillcott in Bristol. The couple had two children – Catherine Mavis, born in 1918, and Beryl, born in 1924. (Catherine was to play an important, though indirect, role in Merrythought's history.) Furthermore evidence that Rendle was employed by Chad Valley no later than November 1922, exists on a Chad Valley patent application of that date, for 'a sound producing device . . . operated from the legs' for use in dolls, toy animals and puppets. The presence of his name on the application suggests he was already a key employee with the firm, and this in turn would suggest he had started working for them some time before 1922.

In all likelihood, had Holmes and Laxton not secured Rendle's services, they would have struggled to get their toy-making venture off the ground. Rendle's own invaluable experience aside, the team of trained workers that followed him (amongst whom was Florence Attwood, Merrythought's first designer whose background is examined in Chapter 3) was vital for the success of the new company. Furthermore, the presence of Rendle may well have persuaded Henry Clarence Janisch, also an experienced toy professional, to defect to Merrythought. Janisch had formerly been responsible for

Death of Toy Factory Director

The managing director of the Merrythought Toy Factory, Iron-Bridge, Mr Clifton James Rendle, Strathmere Haygate Road, Wellington, died shortly after returning home from business on March 31. He was 58.

A native of Weston-super-Mare, Mr. Rendle founded the Iron-Bridge firm in 1930. Previously he was manager of the Chad Valley Toy Works, Wellington, coming to the town after the first world war from the Chad Valley's Birmingham factory. During the 1914-18 war he served in the  North Somerset Yeomanry and was commissioned. In the last war he helped to form the Home Guard in Wellington.

He is survived by his wife and two daughters.

The funeral service was held at Christ Church, Wellington, on Monday, the Rev. J. P. Abbey (vicar) officiating. Family mourners were the widow; Miss B. E Rendle, daughter; Miss R. Rendle, sister; Mr. J. Russell, brother-in-law; Mr. H. Chilcott, nephew; and Mr. L. Hurst (co-director of the factory).

Clifton James Rendle's obituary and photo, published in *Shrewsbury Chronicle*, Friday, 8th April 1949.

sales at J.K. Farnell, a successful Acton-based toy manufacturer which, in 1908, created the first British teddy bear. Janisch's background has proved harder to trace than Rendle's but some information has come to light; when he joined Merrythought he was 37 years old and living in London with his wife, Marion and their 12-year-old son, Duncan. The nationality of Janisch's father is unknown but Janisch himself was born in London's West Ham and moved to Surrey when he was a small boy following the remarriage of his mother. Whether his father died or his parents divorced is unclear.

Both Rendle and Janisch were created directors of the new company, with Rendle in Coalbrookdale looking after production, and Janisch handling sales from the company's showroom at 113, Holborn. Although both were to play a critical role in getting Merrythought off the ground, Rendle was the man on the spot and as such was responsible for driving momentum and setting the tone of the new business.

With the key personnel in place, it was time to find suitable premises for the business and since Rendle lived in Wellington, it made sense to look for something in that locality. Operations began in hired rooms at The Station Hotel in Wellington, until more suitable premises were found at a promising site in Coalbrookdale, a small town situated just a few miles from Wellington. Hailed

Merrythought's first premises at Coalbrookdale.

by many as the birthplace of the Industrial Revolution, Coalbrookdale is known today as Ironbridge. It was here, in 1709, that Abraham Darby first devised the revolutionary process of smelting iron with coke, an innovation that led to the area becoming the most important iron-making centre in the world. Seventy years later, the town attracted further attention when Darby's grandson, Abraham Darby III, built the famous Iron Bridge over the River Severn.

In September 1930 Merrythought was incorporated at Companies House with a nominal capital of £5,000, and production began with a workforce of twenty. Then in February 1931 Merrythought moved into the permanent premises at the site of the old Coalbrookdale iron foundry on the banks of the River Severn. Redolent with history, it is easy to imagine how the site would have provided an inspiring location in which to start up a new business enterprise. However, it seems at least one of the parties involved may have harboured doubts about the venture's ultimate success, because Rendle chose not to move from his home in Wellington until 1934, four years after Merrythought was launched. Only when the business was firmly established did he relocate the few miles from Haygate Road, Wellington to Oswald House, Church Road, Coalbrookdale. Even then, though, the move was temporary because Rendle was back in Haygate Road by 1936 and there he remained until his death in 1949, so perhaps he simply preferred living in Wellington.

Why Merrythought?

Until now, nobody has been able to come up with a plausible explanation for the choice of the new company's name. It undoubtedly has an appealing, child-friendly ring to it, but then so do many other words that might have been chosen. In his book *The Magic of Merrythought*, author John Axe states that nobody remembers why the name was chosen. That may be so, but back in 1939 Clifton Rendle was able to give a very lucid explanation to the trade publication, *Games and Toys*. Apparently, several names had originally been suggested but all were eliminated after Rendle came across the line, 'Tis a *merry thought*' whilst reading a volume of Shakespeare.

Of course, it is fairly well known that 'merrythought' is an old-fashioned, alternative name for the wishbone, the forked bone lying between the breast and neck of a chicken or other fowl. Since Roman times the wishbone has been associated with fortune, and since the Seventeenth Century, perhaps even earlier, the custom of two people pulling this bone with their little fingers has been thought to bring good luck to the one who receives the larger part when the bone breaks. It seems that Rendle liked the line from Shakespeare and its implied suggestion of good fortune so much that he decided Merrythought should be the name of the fledgling toy company. After all, with the mohair spinners' and weavers' businesses in decline, they needed all the help they could get.

Shakespearian quotations aside, however, there is a strong likelihood that both Gordon Holmes and Rendle himself already knew of other businesses that used the Merrythought name. Although Gordon Holmes' family lived in Bingley in Yorkshire, they had a second home in Udimore, a village in East Sussex, where they spent much of their time. The nearest town to Udimore is Rye, located just three miles away. According to Rye Castle Museum, a gift shop called The Merrythought existed in the town for several decades and was there in the 1920s, just before Merrythought began producing toys. As a regular visitor to the Rye area, Holmes may well have been familiar with the shop. As for Rendle, as an inhabitant of Wellington, there is a strong probability that he knew of a café called The Merry Thought which had opened in the town in the late 1920s. He must have been aware of the café and possibly even enjoyed a meal there occasionally. So it seems that the origins of the Merrythought name came from Shakespeare, perhaps with a little help from a small town gift shop and a provincial café.

Keeping it in the family

Merrythought has frequently been referred to in the press as a third generation family business, a phrase that suggests an uninterrupted succession from founding father to son, and then on again to his son. While this is true in essence, it's not quite as clear cut as it sounds. For one thing, the Laxtons – one half of the two founding dynasties – did not play a prolonged role in the company's rich history. George H. Laxton died in 1956 and according to his grandson, John Laxton, the Laxton family's interest in Merrythought faded away some time after that. Even before then, however, neither Holmes or Laxton involved themselves in the day-to-day running of Merrythought. Having secured seasoned toy professionals Rendle and Janisch to guide their enterprise, Holmes and Laxton focused on their other business interests. This assertion is supported by Kenneth D. Brown who, while paying tribute in his book *The British Toy Industry* to Walter Lines of the famous Lines Brothers company, also acknowledges 'more modest empire-builders such as A.C. Janisch (sic) and C. J. Rendle at Merrythought'. The point is that Janisch and Rendle are described as the empire-builders, not Holmes and Laxton.

While the Laxton interest in Merrythought gradually diminished, the reverse was true of the Holmes family, although it was not until the late 1940s that one of them became seriously involved in its day-to-day running. In 1936, Henry Janisch left Merrythought for reasons as yet unknown; Companies

House records state he retired but since he was 43 at the time, that seems unlikely. Following Janisch's departure, Rendle was joined by William Leo Hirst, the son-in-law of Mr Dyson, from Dyson Hall & Co. This hierarchy continued unchanged for over a decade until Gordon Holmes' oldest son, Bernard Trayton Holmes (commonly known as Trayton) came to work at Merrythought in the late 1940s. Some accounts say he joined in 1948 while others put it at 1949; the latter date would certainly make sense because that was the year that Clifton Rendle, the firm's existing Managing Director, died.

According to Oliver Holmes, current MD of Merrythought and son of Trayton, his father had been destined for a career in the Yorkshire textile industry but then the Second World War intervened. The war turned things topsy-turvy for many people and in its aftermath it was not uncommon for individuals to find their lives following paths they had not expected to take. Thus it was for Trayton Holmes who moved from Yorkshire to set up his career and family life in Shropshire, and thus it was that almost twenty years after it had been founded, Merrythought truly became a family-run business. For although his father co-founded the company, it is really from Trayton's arrival onwards that the Merrythought story can be said to have been shaped by the forceful, enterprising, intriguing and occasionally eccentric Holmes family.

The Holmes family history

The names of Trayton and Oliver Holmes are familiar to all Merrythought aficionados but surprisingly, very little has been written about their family background. Considering how strongly the Holmeses are identified with their products, this seems something of an oversight. By contrast, another soft toy dynasty, the German Steiff family, has a very well-documented history which has fostered a strong attachment to the key Steiff figures, so much so that in the family's home town of Giengen in Germany, virtually a secondary industry centred around the heritage of Steiff has sprung up. Visitors are able to visit the restored home of founder Margarete Steiff, where they can see her wheelchair (she was left an invalid after contracting polio as an infant) and sewing machine, while at the state-of-the-art World of Steiff museum a few hundred yards away they can see the actual workbench used by Richard Steiff, one of Margarete's nephews and the man who created the world's first jointed soft toy bear. It is even possible to visit the church where Margarete was baptised. The influx of Steiff tourists has been hugely beneficial to both the Giengen economy and the Steiff company, but the point is that the tourists would not be coming if the characters who created and developed the company had not been made real to the worldwide army of teddy bear enthusiasts through a series of books and articles. Perhaps, therefore, it is time to take a close look at the background and personality of William Gordon Holmes in order to breathe life into what has until now been no more than a name.

Gordon Holmes was one of eight children born to Alfred Holmes, a brewer with his own business near Bingley in Yorkshire, and Kate Kenward, the daughter of a farmer and hop merchant from Icklesham in Sussex. The fourth of five sons, he was educated at Haileybury, a minor public school in Hertfordshire, as was his younger brother Robert. Alfred Holmes maintained two homes, one a large house with considerable grounds located in the environs of Bingley near his brewery, and the other a farm in Udimore, Sussex. From this it is apparent that the family was at least reasonably prosperous and possibly rather more than that.

It seems Gordon and his siblings – Joseph, Mary, Effie, Alfred, Reginald, Robert and Dorothy – had an idyllic childhood, spending their holidays at Udimore which they adored. Alfred reportedly had a violent temper but was nevertheless a good father. Although successful as a businessman and farmer, he could be duped, as when he purchased a healthy-looking cow only to discover when he brought the animal home that its tail had been stuck on.

Alfred died in 1902 aged just 53, leaving his widow, herself severely troubled by rheumatoid arthritis, to bring up the youngest children on her own. Gordon was 17 at the time and just finishing his schooling at Haileybury. Family testimony has it that Gordon was subjected to fairly relentless teasing by some of his older siblings, which although done affectionately may still have left its mark. This might have some bearing on his impulse to make his way as a businessman at such a relatively young age, since it is not unusual for those who have experienced the rough end of familial horseplay to want to prove themselves outside the family unit. What he did between 1902 and 1907, when the partnership with Laxton was established, is unclear, but he probably returned to Bingley to give support and comfort to his mother. He was certainly in the area when he met and fell in love with Marion Nathan, the pretty, auburn-haired daughter of a Bradford export merchant. Gordon and Marion became engaged to be married but then Marion had a change of heart and called the engagement off. Some members of the Holmes family disapproved of the match and were relieved when the engagement ended but their relief was short-lived. No sooner had the heartbroken Gordon bought a red and white cow and named her Marion, in an attempt to soothe his hurt feelings, than the indecisive young lady changed her mind again, and the engagement was back on. They eventually married in 1912, living first in Bingley and later in Ilkley. The marriage produced three children – Joan Rebecca, Bernard Trayton, born just before Gordon left for the front, and Charles Brian.

During the war, Gordon served as a signaller, eschewing the commission he would easily have obtained as an old Haileyburian. (His near contemporary and fellow Haileyburian, Clement Attlee, who later became Prime Minister and like Holmes came from a middle-class background, experienced no difficulty in gaining a commission in 1914.) This apparent reluctance to become an officer suggests a character lacking in self-confidence, or perhaps one uncomfortable with responsibility, although his early foray into the business world would seem to contradict this supposition. In any case, witnessing the carnage of the Western Front Gordon Holmes must have doubted that he would survive the war; indeed, he is

Gordon Holmes (second from front) in recreational mode.

known to have commented to family, with masterful understatement, that the prospects for signallers were not good. However, survive he did, obtaining his discharge from service in December 1918.

Little is known of his personal life after the war but occasional vignettes paint a picture of an energetic, slightly comical character with shades of Kenneth Grahame's Mr Toad. According to family legend he played golf 'with application but no great skill' and was 'a little ungainly . . . there was some doubt as to which way his knees were going to bend'. Ungainliness notwithstanding, he was a keen walker and according to James Laxton, frequently walked to work from Ilkley – a round trip of twelve miles. He was also a determined and enthusiastic driver of small cars, and once rounded a corner straight into a flock of white hens. The air filled with feathers but Holmes could see no casualties so he proceeded on his way. On arrival at his office, a perplexed foreman approached him to ask what should be done with the hen perching on the back axle. The anecdote needs only a 'poop-poop' to make the resemblance to Mr Toad complete.

When George H. Laxton died in 1956, Holmes, Laxton & Co. was run by Gordon Holmes and Laxton's son, another George. Then, ten years later, Holmes retired and moved to Canada where his brother and sister had been living for some years. He died in British Columbia in 1969, aged 84.

CHAPTER TWO

Getting Started
(Life in the 1930s)

ON THE FACE of it, launching a brand new toy-making venture in 1930
demonstrated a degree of bravery verging on the reckless. This was
because in October 1929 the world economy went into freefall
following the collapse of the New York stock market, an event known as the
Wall Street Crash. Millions of dollars were lost as share prices crashed and
although the immediate brunt of the economic disaster was born by the USA,
its repercussions were felt all over the world. In Britain, the crisis led to the
collapse of the country's first Labour government, headed by Ramsay
MacDonald, followed by the formation of a 'National' coalition government
made up of all three major parties, with MacDonald remaining Prime
Minister.

For commerce, the consequences of the crash were very severe, with traditional industries such as ship-building, steel and coal-mining receiving the
worst blows. Unemployment soared, rising from 1.5 million in January 1930
to nearly 3 million in January 1933. Life for the unemployed was very grim;
unemployment benefit did exist but it was scarcely enough to support a
family, and conditions were made harder when the government cut benefit
by ten per cent in 1931. However, even for those lucky enough to be in employment life could be a struggle, since low wages and large families meant the
money seldom spread far enough.

Like so many other industries, the toy trade went through a decidedly rocky
period at the start of the 1930s. Manufacturers, wholesalers and retailers all
saw their profits slump; many found themselves unable to weather the storm
and went into receivership. The most prominent casualty of the period was
Hamleys, the best known toy retailer in the country, which went into liquidation in 1931 owing nearly £160,000, a vast sum in those days. (The shop was
subsequently bought by Lines Brothers, its major creditor.) If an established
business such as Hamleys was unable to survive the recession, what chance

was there for Merrythought, a new toy-making operation with no track record to recommend it to customers? Either the founders were optimists of the highest order, believing they could beat the downward trend, or else the need to find a market for their surplus mohair plush superseded all other considerations. In either case, the choice of the word 'Merrythought', a traditional symbol of good luck, takes on greater significance since the company was going to need all the good luck it could get.

If the country was struggling economically, it wasn't faring much better politically. The problems of unemployment and recession saw people looking to their leaders for solutions, and when the only solutions offered were stringent cutbacks of the 'it has to get worse before it gets better' variety, many became dissatisfied with the traditional parties and looked for alternatives. The British Union of Fascists (BUF), led by Oswald Mosley, took inspiration from the rise of Nazism in Germany while the Communists believed Stalin's regime in Russia held the key to Britain's future. Neither party gained much more than a toe-hold in British politics but they proved very attractive to those who felt let down by the establishment. Then, when Germany started an aggressive programme of rearmament in the mid-1930s, new tensions developed between those who believed the only answer was to appease Hitler in order to preserve the peace, and those who wanted to stand up to him, by military means if necessary.

Unemployment, recession, political tension and the prospect of war over-shadowing everything – this is the familiar portrait of Britain in the 1930s. And yet historians have already re-evaluated the decade and have come to the conclusion that things were not as bad as the picture suggests. While traditional industry was suffering, job opportunities were doubling in new or growing industries such as the motor trade and electrical engineering. At the same time, more people were moving into the middle classes, with a growth in demand for professional and clerical workers. It is true that wages fell between 1929 and 1933 when the country was feeling the impact of the depression but they rose again thereafter, attaining a level twice as high in 1938 as they had been in 1913. More importantly, the cost of living fell by a third between 1920 and 1939, meaning that in real terms, wages were much higher than they seemed. This gentle prosperity saw families on moderate incomes buying their own homes with cheap mortgages, enjoying weekly trips to 'the pictures' and listening to the latest tunes on their new, mass-produced gramophone players and radios. Even for the unemployed, conditions were better than they had been ten years earlier, thanks to new unemployment insurance, pensions and a greater availability of council housing. Admittedly some people did still live in abject poverty, but their numbers were dwindling.

The situation in the toy trade echoed what was happening in society at large. Once the after-shocks of the Wall Street Crash had abated, the industry picked itself up, shrugged off the debris and proceeded to rebuild. While many fell by the wayside – in *The British Toy Business*, Kenneth D. Brown states that 46 per cent of the toy concerns existing in 1930 had gone by the end of the decade – most of the established firms proved strong enough to withstand the economic downturn. The teddy bear and soft toy manufacturers seem to have fared better than most, with the leading players such as J.K. Farnell, Chad Valley and Chiltern all embarking on expansion projects of one sort or another during the troubled period of 1929 to 1933. Searching for a market for their mohair, the Merrythought founders might well have seen more than a flicker of hope in the survival of these firms under such trying economic circumstances. Certainly, it was not unusual for firms in other manufacturing fields to diversify into the toy trade. Waddington's did it in the 1920s when they made the change from printing theatre programmes to producing playing cards (and later board games), as did the Premo Rubber Company in 1935 when it switched from manufacturing rubber shoe heels to making Minibrix construction kits.

Finding a market

In order to sustain a healthy toy market, a significant part of the population needs to have sufficient income to pay for the necessities of life and then have some left over for non-essentials. Surprising as it may seem, these conditions existed in the 1930s because while many of the workforce were grappling with the harsh realities of unemployment, many others were finding themselves better off than ever before. In the early part of the decade, an unskilled worker earned a minimum of £2/10s a week, with a more skilled colleague earning around £3/5s. Meanwhile, in 1930, someone in a clerical or professional occupation earned a weekly income of about £4/15s.

The first page of the first Merrythought catalogue, published in 1931, shows the Merrythought name flanked on one side by 'Quality' and 'Economy', and on the other by 'Courtesy' and 'Service'. While 'Quality', 'Courtesy' and 'Service' are attributes any reputable business would aspire to, the inclusion of the word 'Economy' was perhaps a sign of the times, but did the prices really justify use of the term? Within that first catalogue, the cheapest teddy bear – a 12.5-inch Magnet Bear, described proudly as 'a really cheap line' – is priced at 42 shillings per dozen (which works out at three shillings and sixpence per bear), an affordable amount for all but the very poor. However, for the most expensive bear in the catalogue – a 26-inch Merrythought Bear made from either bronze or 'Sunkiss' mohair, and described as 'feather-light and beautifully finished' – the asking price is 18 shillings each. Allowing for the fact that these were wholesale prices (as indicated by the price quoted per dozen) the figures suggest that from the start, Merrythought intended their products to reach two different types of market; the 'really cheap' Magnet Bears were targeted at the employed working classes while the luxurious Merrythought Bears were intended for the more prosperous middle classes. The high price of the 26-inch Merrythought Bear makes this abundantly clear: at its wholesale price of 18 shillings, it already cost over a third of an unskilled worker's weekly wage, but its retail cost would be around twice that amount, maybe more, taking it way beyond the reach of those on low incomes.

Apart from the teddy bears, the Magnet range in that first catalogue also offered: Rex, a standing dog made from wool plush in three sizes; Baba, a woolly lamb available in four sizes and 'baby colours'; and Twink, a 'Cubby Dog' made in five sizes in 'modern colours, feather-light, soft and different'. (Although described as a Cubby Dog, the catalogue image of Twink looks more koala than canine.) All three were priced at the low end of the market, as were several other toy animal designs, including a pup called Billie and an unnamed wool duck which, in its smallest size, cost just over one shilling,

5

MERRYTHOUGHT

THE MERRYTHOUGHT BEAR.

The B1021 range in Gold or " Sunkiss " (the latest colour) is unequalled for quality and price. Feather-light and beautifully finished—it commands an exceptional sale. The S1021 Series is covered in the highest quality British made art silk plush in assorted colours but the quality and finish are the same as the B1021 series. The colours, Salmon, Ciel, Myosotis, Iris, Canary, Crimson, Copper-glow and Jade are the 1931 selections of the Paris Dress designers.

No.	Price Mohair	No.	Price Art Silk	Approx. Height.
B1021/3	54/- per doz.	S1021/3	60/- per doz.	13"
B1021/4	6/- each	S1021/4	6/8 each	14"
B1021/5	7/- ,,	S1021/5	8/- ,,	15"
B1021/6	8/- ,,	S1021/6	9/- ,,	16"
B1021/7	9/6 ,,	S1021/7	10/8 ,,	17"
B1021/8	11/- ,,	S1021/8	12/8 ,,	18"
B1021/9	12/- ,,	S1021/9	13/4 ,,	19"
B1021/10	13/4 ,,	S1021/10	16/- ,,	21"
B1021/11	16/- ,,			24"
B1021/12	18/- ,,			26"

Nos. 3 and 4 are squeaking ; No. 5 upwards fitted best quality squeeze growls.

THE MAGNET BEAR.

A really cheap line—Gold or Colours.

No.	Approx. Height.	Price.
M1006/3	12¼"	42/- per doz.
M1006/5	15½"	6/- each
M1006/8	19½"	7/6 ,,
M1006/11	24"	11/- ,,

Nos. 5, 8 and 11 fitted automatic growl.

Magnet and Merrythought Bear as advertised in the very first catalogue.

wholesale. But although there was no shortage of more affordable options in that first catalogue, the very fact that certain items were singled out as 'cheap' indicates that Merrythought expected the greater part of their products would be bought by the more affluent members of society. This is made even clearer in a statement printed across the first page of the 1932 catalogue, in which they make it plain that they do not supply their products for coupon gift schemes (which were an early form of consumer loyalty reward). The prominence given to the statement, and the emphatic way in which it is made, infers that Merrythought considered themselves above such schemes (which were meant to appeal to the less prosperous). Inside the catalogue, there is further proof that the firm is targeting the well-to-do, with the appearance of a range of staggeringly expensive jungle animals. The costliest of these was a 30-inch sitting leopard priced at 82 shillings (£4/2s) a piece, not far off the entire weekly income for a typical middle-class earner. Even more expensive were the new 'wheel toys', the largest of which – a 40-inch donkey – cost 103 shillings (£5/3s). Nevertheless, the catalogue still attempted to cater for all pockets, offering a few much cheaper items including a 12-inch Merrythought Bear in light gold mohair at 36 shillings per dozen (that's three shillings each), a 9-inch white wool plush lamb at 27 shillings per dozen (two shillings and threepence each) and 'Quacka', a 5-inch yellow art silk duck priced at 21 shillings per dozen (one shilling and ninepence each).

Competition and customers

Although Merrythought was very much a newcomer to the soft toy market in 1930s Britain, it managed to make a big impact in a very short period, thanks largely to the experience Rendle, Florence Attwood and Janisch brought from Chad Valley and J.K. Farnell. These companies were renowned for the quality of their products and were well respected in the industry. By the time the first Merrythought toys went into production, Chad Valley had been creating teddy bears for fifteen years. Farnell's track record was even more impressive; they had made the first British teddy bear back in 1908, had been supplying Harrods with teddy bears since 1910, and in 1921 a Farnell bear bought from the world-famous department store became the inspiration for A.A. Milne's *Winnie the Pooh* stories.

When production started at Merrythought, Rendle and his team of former Chad Valley workers were able to draw on their knowledge of Chad Valley designs to get going immediately. While some of the earliest Merrythought products showed true originality, others – notably the teddy bears – have elements that clearly indicate a Chad Valley/Farnell influence. Proportions and shapes often mirrored Chad Valley designs, while the most obvious 'borrowing' from Farnell was their webbed claw stitching, although where

There are similarities between this early Merrythought bear and the 1930s Chad Valley example shown below.

Farnell's webbed claw stitching with five claws.

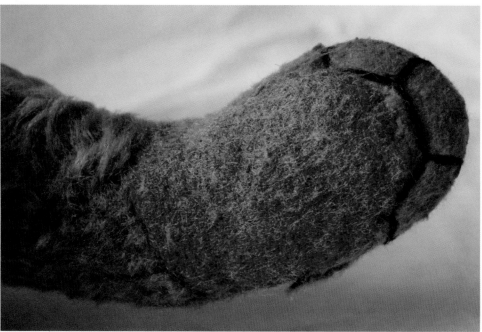

Merrythought's webbed stitching with four claws.

Farnell used five claws, Merrythought used just four. It seems a little odd today but at the time it was common – albeit unofficial – practice for soft toy manufacturers to draw design inspiration from their competitors. In any case, it is hardly surprising that some of Florence Attwood's Merrythought designs were Chad Valley influenced since that was where she had honed her designing skills.

While Rendle ensured top quality toys came out of the factory, Janisch used his considerable sales experience, gleaned at J.K. Farnell, to find a market for them. As it turned out, such was the demand for the new company's products that the total number of toys offered in the catalogue (including every permutation of size and material) grew from 150 plus in 1931 to 350 plus in

This later Merrythought teddy was an exclusive for John Lewis.

NOVELTIES
IN SOFT TOYS, ETC.
Including a Full Range of

Cats, Rabbits, Dogs, Donkeys, Bears, etc.

When in London for the
B.I.F. do not fail to visit us

W. H. JONES
8 & 10 Great Arthur Street
LONDON

One minute from Aldersgate Street Station

An ad for W.H. Jones which appeared in *Games and Toys* trade journal in 1929.

1932. To the competition the message was loud and clear – Merrythought meant business.

If the Merrythought founders regarded Chad Valley and Farnell as their main rivals, (if only because they were able to use what they knew about these successful companies to give them a head start in the trade), they had other significant competitors. From the domestic market these included H.G. Stone & Co. (better known by their 'Chiltern Toys' trade name), Dean's, W.H. Jones, Ealontoys and Norah Wellings, while overseas competition came mainly from leading German firms such as Margarete Steiff GmbH. Very few American-made teddy bears were sold in Britain, the American manufacturers preferring to concentrate their sales efforts on their home territory. Without access to detailed financial records for these companies (many of which have been lost or destroyed over the years) it is impossible to accurately assess the inroads Merrythought made into their competitors' profits. However, the fact that the firm's staff had grown from twenty workers in 1930 to 200 by 1939 suggests a degree of success that would be considered praiseworthy today, and was little short of extraordinary in the financially uneasy 1930s. One competitor, W.H. Jones, did not fare so well, going into voluntary liquidation in 1937 even though, having started trading some twelve years before Merrythought, its chances of survival might have been considered better than the newcomer's.

A further measure of Merrythought's success is found in the quality of the retailers that sold its products. Today, you are most likely to discover Merrythought creations on sale within the many specialist teddy bear shops found across the country, but in the past, Harrods, Hamleys, Selfridges and John Lewis have all been happy to have Merrythought teddies and toys on their shelves, as have many other quality outlets including independent department stores, leading toy shops and upmarket gift retailers.

Chapter Three

Stars of the Early Years (1930–1939)

Florence Attwood: first lady of Merrythought

WITH VERY FEW exceptions, all the products produced by Merrythought from 1930 until 1948 were designed by Florence Attwood. During this period, it is her name that appears on the front page of the factory's 'trial book' which records details of new designs, including those that never progressed beyond the experimental stage, as well as those that made it into the Merrythought range. Like any commercial designer, however, Florence would have had to pay attention to the wishes of her superiors – in this case Rendle and Janisch – while the assistant she is known to have had may also have dropped an idea in here and there. Furthermore, when tasked with creating an entire range from scratch, it is inconceivable that she would not have used her knowledge of Chad Valley designs to give her a head start. Acknowledging this does not in any way lessen Florence's achievements; she created enough commercially successful designs (many of which were highly innovative) to ensure Merrythought survived through the difficult early years and beyond. What makes her success in the high pressure environment of a fledgling toy factory especially impressive is the fact that she was deaf, since attitudes to people with disabilities were far less enlightened in the 1930s than they are today.

Until now, precious little has been known about Florence Attwood's personal circumstances beyond the fact that she was deaf (or even a 'deaf mute' according to some sources) and that she started her career working for Chad Valley, having met Clifton Rendle's daughter at a school in Manchester. In reality Florence was not mute but, having lost her hearing following a bout of measles at the age of two, her speech had an unusual cadence of which she was aware, and for this reason she often chose to communicate by sign language or by writing things down. She was born in Shropshire in 1907 and her parents, Walter – an iron foundry worker – and Sarah, had several other children. The opportunity to raise herself above these fairly humble origins came, ironically, as a result of her deafness; in 1915 she was offered a place at the Royal Schools for the Deaf in Manchester, an institution founded in 1823. Due to leave the school in 1923, instead Florence was chosen to stay on as one of the first pupils in a newly opened vocational training department where she learned dressmaking, the skill that was to shape her future. About two years later, another deaf girl from Shropshire started at the Manchester school and although she was quite a lot younger than Florence, the two became friendly, perhaps as a result of travelling together from Shropshire to Manchester. The younger girl was Catherine Mavis Rendle, daughter of Clifton Rendle, who at that time was working in a senior position at Chad Valley in Wellington. When Florence completed her training in 1926, Rendle repaid the friendship she had shown his daughter by employing her as a toy maker and designer, and when he left to set up Merrythought, she loyally followed him. That loyalty was repaid when her father lost his job at the iron foundry and work was found for him at Merrythought, making wooden, zinc-bound patterns from Florence's designs. Sometime around 1948 Florence Attwood became ill and had to leave Merrythought. She died in 1952, not 1949 as has previously been suggested, at the age of 44.

Although this seems little enough to know about the woman responsible for creating some of the world's best-loved teddy bear and toy designs, it is significantly more than has previously been known. Having lived such a tragically short life, it is fitting that Florence Attwood's name lives on through her work. The following section highlights all her significant bear designs produced during the 1930s, as well as some more obscure examples.

1931: Magnet, Merrythought, Tumpy and Bingie

In 1931, Merrythought produced its first catalogue, offering thirty-three different soft toy designs. Dogs dominated the catalogue, with fourteen separate dog designs on offer, while rabbits were in second place with seven designs. Surprising as it must seem to those for whom the Merrythought name means teddies, only four bear designs appeared in that first catalogue, although the main two – the Magnet and the Merrythought – were offered in so many different permutations of size, material and colour that the actual number of bears potentially available was far greater than this.

The Magnet Bear was described as 'A really cheap line' and was made in a choice of gold or colours. It was available in four sizes – 12.5, 15.5, 19.5 and 24 inches – and all but the 12.5-inch bear had an automatic growl. This size cost 42 shillings per dozen while for the 24-inch, the catalogue price was 11 shillings each.

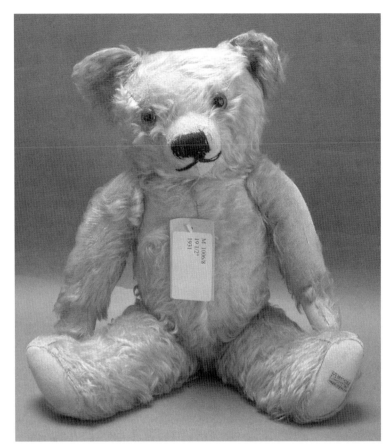

The label on this 19.5-inch bear from Merrythought's archives identifies it as a 1931 Magnet.

At the luxury end of the market there was the Merrythought Bear which came in two ranges. First, there was the B1021 range, made from mohair and described as 'feather-light and beautifully finished'. The B1021 colour choices were Gold or Sunkiss, described in the catalogue as 'the latest colour', and there were ten size options: 13, 14, 15, 16, 17, 18, 19, 21, 24 and 26 inches. The 13 and 14-inch bears had squeakers while all the others were fitted with 'best quality squeeze growls'. Prices for the B1021 range started at 54 shillings per dozen for the 13-inch bears, rising to 18 shillings each for the 26-inch.

Slightly more expensive were the bears in the S1021 range. They were made from art silk (artificial silk) plush, the very first man-made fibre, which had been around since the late Nineteenth Century but was new to the toy industry. Today it seems strange that an artificial material should have cost more than a natural one but at the time art silk was regarded as a luxury item. One of the benefits of art silk was that it could be produced in a variety of decidedly unbearlike colours. The catalogue description for the S1021 states that the series is 'covered in the highest quality British-made art-silk plush in assorted colours but the quality and finish are the same as the B1021 series'. According to the catalogue, the colour choices – Salmon, Ciel, Myosotis, Iris, Canary, Crimson, Copper-glow and Jade – were the selection of the 1931 Paris dress designers. This is interesting because it highlights the fact that at the time, some women saw teddy bears as amusing fashion accessories, in much the same way that others regarded small dogs (and still do today) as style statements. Matching the bear to her outfit would have been essential for a smart woman-about-town. The sizes of the S1021 were the same as for the B1021, with the exception that there were no 24 and 26-inch options.

While the Magnet and Merrythought Bears were traditional teddy designs

Catalogue illustration of Tumpy.

19-inch bear made from green artificial silk plush.

that were probably intended for older children (and even adults, in the case of the S1021 series), the other two bear designs from the 1931 catalogue were designed to appeal to infants. Described as 'The Merrythought Bear Cubs', their qualities of softness and cuddliness were emphasised. Tumpy, a delightful design that looks ahead of its time, was hailed as 'The baby Bear Cub that appeals, appeals, and appeals!' It was made in soft woolly plush, in a variety of 'dainty' colours, and was 'feather-light, soft and most attractive'. Tumpy came in three sizes – 12, 14.5 and 17 inches – and the prices were similar to those for the B1021 Merrythought Bear.

Given that Tumpy was an innovative and appealing design, his reign in the Merrythought catalogue was strangely short-lived, reappearing in 1932 but vanishing for good thereafter. By contrast, the second 'Merrythought Bear Cub' to feature in the 1931 catalogue fared considerably better. Bingie, a 'Sitting Cub' made from brown and white curly plush, was jointed at the head and arms but not the legs. The 1931 catalogue, in which Bingie is available in three sizes from 9 to 14 inches, describes Bingie as 'cuddley (sic) and winsome'. In the 1932 catalogue, he is called 'A Merrythought best seller' and is available in three further size options – 16 and 19 inches – as well as the oddly unspecific 'a good show piece'. The proud boast in this catalogue was that 'Bingie sells himself' which probably explains why the Bingie name was used to launch two new designs, Cutie Bingie and Baby Bingie.

1932: The bears evolve

Cutie Bingie, available as a 10, 12.5 and 15-inch toy, was part of a new Merrythought range called Movie Toys, a name that has nothing to do with the cinema and everything to do with the fact that the toys had articulated limbs, enabling them to adopt many different poses. So proud were Merrythought of this clever design, claiming somewhat ambitiously that it

Bingie Sitting Cub, 11 inches, in almost mint condition.

would revolutionise the toy trade, that they applied for a patent to protect it. The more advanced Movie Toys could move their heads, legs and tails but the Cutie Series, consisting of six designs (three of which were dogs) was a simpler and cheaper version on which the legs alone were articulated.

While Cutie Bingie was a toy that encouraged imaginative play, Baby Bingie was part of a new series called Teenie Toys which was aimed at the very young and was simply intended to provide babies with a pleasing tactile toy. Indeed, the two sizes in which Baby Bingie was made, 5.5 and 7 inches, were just right for popping in a pram or cot.

Aside from the Bingies, there were other interesting developments in the 1932 catalogue. The Merrythought Bear range now offered four different options: the B1021 series in Light Gold mohair – 'a special soft stuffed line at remarkable prices'; the BX1021 in Old Gold mohair – 'unequalled for quality and price'; the S1021 art silk series with a new assortment of colours, as dictated by the Paris fashion designers; and the Q1021 'Best Quality' series of bears made from long curly piled mohair, described as 'a real aristocrat among bears'. All the ranges were available in sizes from 12 to 26 inches, and there was a significant difference between the cost of the B1021 and Q1021 bears: a 26-inch B1021 cost 16 shillings a piece, the same size Q1021 cost 25 shillings. Along the way, the cheaper Magnet Bear had been dropped completely, suggesting demand for the pricier bears was sufficiently high to justify concentrating on them.

A feature of the 1932 catalogue is that the teddy bears had jumped from page five the previous year to page two, appearing immediately after the title page. It is tempting to read this as an indication of the teddy bear's importance to the young company, but the idea is somewhat quashed by the front cover which features illustrations of a dog, rabbit and cat, but no bear. The notion is further dampened by the fact that in the 1933 catalogue, the first three pages are devoted entirely to dogs, and bears do not make an appearance at all until page six (and even then it's a solitary Cutie Bingie). Perhaps the truth is that, healthy as the market was for teddy bears, Merrythought saw equal or greater potential in other toys and therefore the teddy was just one of several important products. However, the teddy does seem to have served one extremely useful purpose for the company in 1932. An entry in the factory's 'trials book' dated 30th September 1932 reads: 'Special Teddy Bear, height 13 inches, for Harrods'. This is significant because it was probably the first business Merrythought ever did with the famous department store.

In 1932, the fact was that bears of all types, not just teddies, were on the increase. The 1932 catalogue introduced an open-mouthed Laughing Baby Bear; Sammy, a baby polar bear; Bush Baby, a koala-style bear; a Movie Toys polar bear cub and a polar and brown bear on wheels. Laughing Baby Bear, available in three sizes and made from art silk in two different colourways, was described as: 'A new conception of a "toy" bear cub'. In actual fact, a 'laughing' bear with open mouth had been made in the USA as early as 1907, and in the 1920s a German firm made a version of their own. The difference between these earlier designs and Merrythought's version was that the former looked rather scary, due to the inclusion of teeth, whilst toothless Laughing Baby Bear appeared happy and friendly. Perhaps not friendly enough, though, because the mirthful cub had disappeared from the catalogue by 1936.

1933–1935: Dressed Bingies, Bobby Bruin, Dutch Bears and more

The big news on the bear front in 1933 was the proliferation of the Bingie family. Original Bingie, Cutie Bingie and Baby Bingie were still listed, but now they were joined by five dressed Bingie relatives: Sailor, Grenadier, Girl, Boy and Ski-Girl. (Also in the Bingie family, somewhat bizarrely, was Ronnie the Rabbit, dressed in trousers, jersey and shoes.) These Bingies had mohair heads and paws while their bodies were made from cloth. All the bears were available in 15 and 20-inch size options, apart from Grenadier Bingie who, because of his tall busby hat, was either 20 or 27 inches. Due to the absence of the 1934 catalogue, which went astray at some point in Merrythought's history, we don't know for certain what happened to the Bingies that year but the factory's 'trials book' reveals that a Highlander version was designed in January 1934, so it may well have featured in the same year's catalogue. It was certainly there in the 1935 catalogue, along with all the others apart from Ski-Girl who had gone. (It is interesting to note that the Grenadier was now referred to as a Guardsman. This may have been unintentional, a mere slip of the pen, because of course the correct name for a Grenadier is Grenadier Guardsman.) The following year (1936), Girl and Boy Bingie had also departed. Today, dressed Bingies are very popular with collectors, especially those that retain their original clothing. Unsurprisingly, considering her limited run in the catalogue, Ski-Girl is the rarest, closely followed by Girl and Boy.

As for traditional teddies, 1933 saw a dramatic paring down of the Merrythought Bear range. Gone

20-inch Guardsman Bingie.

Highlander Bingie, 20 inches, circa 1935.

Cheap when new, today this blue and pink teddy is something of a rarity.

were the BX1021, S1021 and Q1021 series, leaving just the B1021 in Light Gold Mohair (going up to 30 inches for the first time) and a new series, the F1021, made from curly piled mohair plush and, just like the Q1021 series from 1932, described as 'real aristocrats among bears'. The scope of the 1934 range is unknown but by 1935 the traditional teds were back in force; frustratingly, the relevant pages of the catalogue are missing but the price list remains and it reveals no fewer than six different series of conventional-style teddies. Amongst them are the H range, which is revealed in the following year's catalogue simply to be a new name for the original Merrythought Bear, and the AX series which proves to be a reworking of the Magnet Bear, last seen in 1931.

Some fairly radical new designs made an appearance in 1934 and 1935. Bobby Bruin was a sturdily constructed, charismatic bear with very large feet. He was made with the patented 'Movie' joints and came in three sizes – 17.5, 20.5 and 26 inches. An entry in the 1934 'trials book' seems to allude to him; although it refers to a 'Movie Teddy Bear' rather than Bobby Bruin, the description of a bear with 'Movie frame in legs for sitting position or standing on hams' fits. Oddly enough, Bobby does not appear to have found favour with the public; he reappeared in the 1936 catalogue,

Bobby Bruin, circa 1935.

where he was described as 'Soft and cuddlesome. Golden-brown. Designed from nature', but then he vanished, not appearing again until 1996 (when he was created in a limited edition of 750). Needless to say, original examples of these delightful bears are much sought-after today.

Another newcomer in 1934/1935 was the Dutch Teddy Bear, so-called because its legs were styled to resemble the wide trousers traditionally worn by Dutch boys. This design, with cloth body and mohair head, paws and feet, was available in two unspecified sizes. As for other designs, a note in the 1934 'trials book' introduces the intriguing possibility that Merrythought had been approached by the confectioners, Fox's – famous for their Glacier Mints – to create a toy version of their trademark polar bear. It was to have measured 15.5 inches in a begging position, and would have been made from white

Bobby Bruin in profile, showing the pronounced curve of his elbows.

plush stuffed with mohair. Sadly, whether it was ever commercially produced remains unknown. Meanwhile another 1934 'trials book' design that does not feature in any existing catalogue was put in production; this was a 'Teddy Bear – cheap type' with 'Blue and pink sided body, Nearly straight legs and arms, All woodwool stuffed, 15.5 inches'. Cheap though these bears may have been when they were first made, today they are something of a rarity. Less radical but guaranteed to please was the 1935 introduction of an alpaca Bingie Sitting Cub.

This alpaca and mohair Bingie started out as a nightdress case before being restuffed and sewn up.

1936: Rebranded traditional teds, and Chubby Bear

1936 saw a change of strategy concerning Merrythought's traditional-style teddy bears that was to remain in place until 1939. The number of different series was reduced from the previous year, from six to five, and anyone comparing catalogue illustrations with those from earlier years could be excused a certain amount of confusion. The illustration used in 1931 for the Magnet Bear was now labelled AS and AX. The AS were described as bears 'made of art silk plush in seven beautiful shades – very soft kapok filled' while the AX 'represents the finest Teddy made, in short close-pile old-gold lustrous plush. Very soft stuffed'. It's a far cry from the 'really cheap line' description of the Magnet Bear five years earlier. To further the confusion, the illustration formerly used for the 'unequalled for quality and price' Merrythought Bear was now labelled as the H, a medium length pile gold mohair bear 'produced expressly for the cheap market'. The AX was available in twelve sizes ranging from 10.5 to 26 inches, while the AS came in just seven size options from 12 to 18 inches and the H had a meagre four options, 12, 15, 17 and 21 inches. The

use of the same illustration to identify different bears can cause problems for collectors, which is why Merrythought bears from this period are very often simply referred to as '1930s bears' without reference to a particular series.

Thankfully, the M and T, the two new series joining the AS, AX and H bears in 1936 were given a brand new illustration. The M was filled with soft kapok and 'made of rich gold long pile shaggy pure mohair'. It was said to represent 'Acclaimed unrivalled value' although one can't help but wonder who exactly was acclaiming a product that had only just appeared in the cata-

17-inch bear, 1936–1938, made of red artificial silk plush.

Sweet, 12-inch mohair teddy from the 1930s.

logue. Its fellow newcomer, the T, was made from 'medium novelty, quality long-pile mohair of a biscuit brown-ground colour, tipped with a deeper shade' which was said to give it a 'cubby' effect. Like the AX range, the M was available in twelve different sizes, starting at 12 inches and going up to 30; the number of sizes and the 30-inch option suggest Merrythought were confident of its success, while the five sizes offered for the T – 14, 16, 18, 21 and 26 inches – may indicate they were less sure about it.

Away from the traditional teds, another new boy arrived on the scene in 1936. Chubby Bear was described as 'a new and charming adaptation of the Teddy Bear, yet different'. Featuring head, body, arms and legs made from brown alpaca, with cream alpaca inset muzzle and feet, Chubby was an attractive bear who came in four sizes, 9, 12, 16 and 20 inches. However, his presence in the Merrythought range was to be fleeting as he had vanished by 1937, never to be seen again.

1937: Arrival of Teddy Doofings, Pandas and Bombardier Bruin

For Merrythought, 1937 was arguably the most exciting year of the entire decade in terms of bear developments. For a start, it saw the arrival of Teddy Doofings, surely one of the most extraordinary creations ever to be marketed as a bear. Rumour has it that his designer, Florence Attwood, was strongly influenced by Mickey Mouse when she created him, and it's certainly easy to see similarities. However, there was much more to Teddy Doofings than this; as his page in the catalogue rather breathlessly put it, 'His arms move, his fingers move. His eyes shut and open, all of him is movable. How completely a child can play with "Teddy Doofings"! So much playability has never before been incorporated in a single toy'.

So proud were Merrythought of their new creation that his name, a horrible pun based on the fact that this was a bear that could 'do fings', was patented and registered. Looking at the catalogue, there's a real sense that Merrythought believed the 22-inch Teddy Doofings was going to hit the big time. He appears on page two of the catalogue, before any other product, and the entire page is his alone. He is shown in four separate poses to demonstrate his versatility, and beneath the pictures is an odd little rhyme which exaggerates his abilities somewhat:

> *He can laugh, he can cry*
> *He can sing, he can sigh*
> *He can sweep, he can sleep*
> *He can box and darn socks*
> *He can play any way*

Almost as an afterthought comes the information that Doofings is very soft and is made in brown, blue, pink and green, with a sentence in brackets revealing that brown is the most popular colour. Perhaps surprisingly, he does not feature in the abridged catalogue published by Merrythought later that same year, but he is there again in the 1938 catalogue. As with 1933, there is no catalogue for 1939 but whether it has been lost or was never published is uncertain, although as a supplement was published that year it seems probable that one was produced. Either way, there's no sure way of knowing if Teddy Doofings was still part of the Merrythought range in 1939 but what is certain is that once the Second World War was over, his day had gone. After all the hype, Teddy Doofings turned out to be a three-minute wonder, destined only to make a partial comeback as a smaller, limited edition in the early 1990s. It leaves the unanswerable question, what if the war hadn't intervened? Would Teddy Doofings have brought Merrythought the kind of success they attained with Cheeky, another unusual-looking bear which was to take the toy world by storm in the late 1950s?

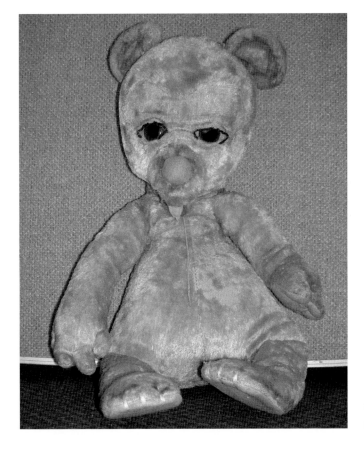

Teddy Doofings was
distinctive but short-lived.

2

MERRYTHOUGHT Teddy Doofings.

(Patented and registered).

His arms move, his fingers move. His eyes shut and open, all of him is movable. How completely a child can play with "Teddy Doofings"! So much playability has never before been incorporated in a single toy.

No. 1622.

Very soft and made in brown, blue, pink and green.
(Brown is the most popular).

He can laugh, he can cry
He can sing, he can sigh
He can sweep, he can sleep
He can box and darn socks
He can play any way.

Send for Show Card.

Copy of 1937 catalogue page announcing the arrival of Teddy Doofings.

Appearing in the 1937 catalogue with far less panoply than Teddy Doofings were three designs inspired by giant pandas. To appreciate the impact these toys made in 1937, it helps to know that until 1936, no giant pandas had been seen outside their native China. Indeed, westerners had not even known of their existence until 1869 when a French missionary was shown the skin of a dead panda. In 1929, Kermit and Theodore Roosevelt Jr., the sons of President Theodore Roosevelt after whom the teddy bear is named, attained the dubious triumph of becoming the first foreigners to shoot a panda, a fact that seems mildly ironic considering their father's association with the teddy bear stemmed from his refusal to shoot a captive bear during a hunting trip. People were gradually becoming more aware of the existence of these exotic, almost mythical creatures and in 1936, an American fashion designer called Ruth Harkness travelled to China intent on bringing a live panda back to the USA. In November of that year she was successful, returning home with a two-month-old panda cub which she named Su-Lin (the cub subsequently became a star attraction at Brookfield Zoo in Chicago).

Bombardier Bruin.

1937 catalogue illustration of Bombardier Bruin.

The press had a field day with the story and word spread as far as Ironbridge, where someone at Merrythought, probably Rendle or Florence Attwood, saw pictures of Su-Lin and cleverly recognised the potential for toy pandas. Initial designs recorded in the 'trials book' in June 1937 were swiftly turned around in time for them to feature in the 1937 catalogue. The Panda Bear, illustrated standing on all fours, was described as being 'modelled from data supplied by an eminent Scientist' while Panda Teddy Bear was heralded as 'a Merrythought exclusive Novelty just added to our range'. Both were made from mohair plush. A helpful explanatory note was provided for any customers not as up to date with world events as the folk at Merrythought: 'The Panda Bear is a native of North Central China, a very rare species and no living specimen yet lives in a Zoo. Our "Panda" Teddy is a "free" adaptation in the ever popular "Teddy Bear" shape'.

By releasing their Panda Teddy in

1937, Merrythought appear to have stolen a march on one of their German rivals, the mighty Steiff company. In *Christie's Century of Teddy Bears*, Leyla Maniera writes of Su-Lin's arrival at a zoo in Chicago in 1937 and states that Steiff launched a black and white jointed panda the following year. Merrythought's reaction to the design opportunity presented by the giant panda was very impressive; they even enlarged and adjusted the Panda Bear design in order to create a third panda offering that year, a Riding 'Panda' Bear which was introduced as part of their extensive Riding Animals range. Having made its debut, the panda toy was about to take the British nursery by storm and with more panda designs on the way, Merrythought were ready to grab their share of the market.

First though, another innovative bear design was about to make his debut in the 1937 catalogue. Intended to appeal to young children, Bombardier Bruin was an unjointed bear made from art silk. Styled in a quasi-military uniform with hat, buttons and braid, he was fitted with a Merrythought invention called Stayput which enabled him to hold a sitting position even though he was unjointed. He was offered in five sizes from 12 to 24 inches high, and a companion animal called Military Mick was also available. Bombardier Bruin made it into the 1938 catalogue but seems to have faded away thereafter. Like Teddy Doofings, he is something of a rarity today.

1938/1939: Going Dutch, Kiddies Kuddly Cubs and more pandas

Having made a brief appearance a few years earlier, the Dutch-style bear returned to the catalogue in 1938, albeit with modifications. This time there were two distinct types of Dutch bear; one, the Dutch Bear, was marketed as part of Merrythought's Soft Dolls and 'Dutch' Toys collection while the other, the Dutch Teddy, was categorised as a novelty teddy bear along with the pandas, Bingies etc. Dutch Bear had a mohair head but the rest of him was made of cloth and he appeared to be fully clothed, although his outfit was not removable. He was able to stand with his paws tucked into the pockets of his wide, Dutch-boy trousers. By contrast, Dutch Teddy was made from alpaca and only his Dutch-style trousers were made from a different material. Dutch Bear was available in three sizes – 11.5, 16 and 21 inches high – while Dutch Teddy had eight size options, starting at 7 and going up to 26.5 inches. Chad Valley were making very similar bears during the 1930s although which company was responsible for the original idea is not known.

With only four pages of the 1939 catalogue supplement to go on, getting a true picture of the range that year is impossible but it is extremely fortunate that the existing pages are mostly concerned with bears. Three delightful new bear designs appeared as part of a range called Kiddies Kuddly Cubs and were further designated as 'The Little Forest Friends' series. Harry Rowntree, a leading children's illustrator of the day, designed three animals for this series including a charming little chap called Bobby the Bear. Bobby had a soft, moulded head and was made from natural alpaca plush. He measured just 8 inches high and had a fitted voice. Also in the Kiddies Kuddly Cubs range, but not designed by Harry Rowntree, were Baby Bruin, 10 inches high, and the imaginatively named Teddie who was 9 inches high. Both were made from alpaca: Baby Bruin in shell pink and Teddie in fawn. The catalogue description states they were 'specially designed for small children. They are of natural shades of alpaca plushes, very soft, fully jointed and fitted voice'.

The last two extant pages of the 1939 supplement show how completely Merrythought believed the future was black and white as far as teddies were concerned. With one exception, every item on the two pages is a variation on the panda theme; that exception is a traditional-style teddy, designated the B.B. Range because of its burnished bronze mohair, which is represented by the illustration used in 1936 for the M and T ranges. Offered in eleven size options ranging from 12 to 26 inches, it comes as a shock to realise it is the only available traditional teddy. Sharing a page with the B.B. is a design called Panda Bear which turns out to be one and the same as Panda Teddy Bear, but available now in eight sizes as opposed to the original five. A note alongside one of the two images of Panda Bear informs that 'Merrythought Panda Toys are approved by and supplied to the London Zoo'. Following the arrival of Su-Lin in the USA a couple of years earlier, a giant panda called Ming had been taken to London Zoo in 1938 and when panda mania duly swept the nation, Merrythought's early association with panda toys stood the company in good stead. Another four panda designs, described as 'Hygienic Panda Toys', were introduced on the next page of the 1939 supplement. Mascot Panda Teddies looked like Panda Bear but were made from art silk and came in two small sizes, 5.5 and 7.5 inches, while

1930s mohair panda, 17 inches, with foot label Reg Design No.821561.

Chummy Panda 'in beautiful plushes, soft and cuddly' had a fitted voice and jointed arms and head. Cuddly Panda Doll was 11.5 inches high and described as 'Ideal as a slumber toy' while 9-inch Panda Glove Toy 'enables one to imitate the Panda's amusing antics', a big claim to make for a glove puppet and an indication of Merrythought's inclination to reinterpret the panda in as many different toy forms as possible. War was on its way but until it arrived, pandas were the big story at Ironbridge in the summer of 1939.

The one that got away

A 1932 Merrythought 'trial book' entry records a design for a Rupert Bear. Standing 14.5 inches high, the bear was dressed in trousers, jersey, scarf and leather boots, with head and paws made from plush, and body and arms made from canvas. Having been a fixture in the *Daily Express* since Mary Tourtel created him in 1920, Rupert would have been a real coup for Merrythought, but it seems nothing came of the design and thus Rupert aficionados had to wait until 1993 for the first Merrythought incarnation of the bear from Nutwood. That is, apart from that first experimental design. What became of it is unknown but should it turn up today, there's no doubt the interest in it would be enormous.

Swastikas and wishbones

Looking at the title page of the 1932 catalogue, which lists the company's addresses, showrooms and various overseas agents, it comes as something of a shock to notice three little swastikas as well as the Merrythought trademark wishbone. Their presence, however, should not be read as a declaration of support for Hitler and the Nazi party, since the emblem had been used for centuries as a symbol of good luck. Furthermore, the fact that the Nazis had appropriated the emblem for use on their flag may not have been widely known in provincial England and even had it been, in 1932 this would not necessarily have been perceived in a negative light. Although Hitler was already on his way to power, his true colours were yet to be perceived by most people and indeed many believed he was just what Germany needed.

In the 1933 catalogue, published when Hitler had become Chancellor, the three swastikas had been reduced to one. We can't know if it appeared in 1934 as the catalogue for this year is missing, as is most of 1935's. However, by 1936, when the prospect of war was beginning to cast a long shadow across Europe, the swastika had vanished from Merrythought catalogues for good.

CHAPTER FOUR

A Brave New World (1940–1959)

———⟫◆⟪———

Fortunes of war

FOR MILLIONS of people, normal life came to a halt in September 1939 with the start of the Second World War. When it finished, in August 1945, those attempting to resume their lives as before were to discover that everything had changed. British servicemen returning home found cities devastated by bomb damage and a civilian population grappling with the daily challenges of rationing. Although everyone agreed that Winston Churchill had done a remarkable job in steering Britain during the war years, the popular consensus was that a new leader was needed to rebuild the country. Many believed that having served their country unflinchingly throughout the war, the ordinary working people of Britain now deserved a better deal and Labour's proposed cradle-to-grave welfare state offered just that. In the General Election of 1945, Labour won a landslide victory over the Conservatives and despite his status as national hero, Churchill was replaced as Prime Minister by Clement Attlee. It was the start of a brave new world in which social barriers were gradually broken down and, for better or worse, the formal manners and rigid conventions of the pre-war era gave way to the relaxed, laissez-faire attitudes of today.

At Merrythought, too, much had changed, or was about to. During the war, the Admiralty sequestered the Ironbridge factory premises, using them for map-making and storage, and many employees left to take up different types of war work. In 1939, 200 people had worked at Merrythought but when the company rented temporary premises in Wellington, only eight remained. Even with such a drastically reduced workforce and with materials in increasingly short supply, the company initially attempted to continue making toys. The 'trial book' shows that Florence Attwood came up with a number of patriotic designs including dolls dressed as soldiers, sailors, ATS (Auxiliary

Territorial Service) members and Red Cross nurses. She also recorded details of a new Bingie dressed in the skirt, hat and coat of the ATS but it is unclear if the design was ever produced commercially. By 1942, however, the 'trial book' entries ended as the depleted Merrythought personnel set to making essential war items such as helmet linings, gas-mask bags and uniform chevrons. (There is some evidence to suggest that Merrythought combined its toy-making expertise with this war work in order to create a child's gas-mask bag with a teddy on the front. A 'trial book' entry for March 1941 refers to 'Teddy, American cloth trousers, attached to small respirator case. Height 12 inches'. There is no proof that Merrythought ever put the cases into production but from time to time gas-mask bags with teddies on the front do crop up at auction and although, alas, all have so far been unlabelled, the trial book entry at least raises the possibility that they were manufactured by Merrythought. Perhaps one day a labelled example will be found to settle the matter once and for all.)

The war ended in August 1945 but even then, circumstances ensured that life at Merrythought was never going to be the same again. Toy production restarted in 1946 when the company went home to Ironbridge and new workers were taken on, but these attempts to rebuild the company's fortunes were initially hampered by the shortage of supplies and also by severe damage caused by the worst flood the River Severn had experienced in recorded history. Worse was to follow a year or so later when Florence Attwood developed a serious illness, believed to be cancer. As her condition worsened she became unable to work and finally left Merrythought in 1949. The same year, the ultimate blow fell when Clifton Rendle died shortly after returning home from a business trip. Gordon Holmes' son, Trayton, stepped in to fill the gap left by Rendle's death, but a new chief designer, Jean Barber, was not appointed until 1952. As the decade progressed, Merrythought began slowly to adjust to the changing times, largely thanks to the efforts of Trayton Holmes and Jimmy Matthews (see Movers and Shakers, below). One obvious manifestation of change was the makeover the catalogue was given. In 1958, for the first time, a selection of the company's products appeared on the front cover while inside changes were made, as the catalogue copy explained, 'so that you can more easily see our range, which in turn makes ordering easier'. Those words are significant as they indicate that Merrythought were becoming more sophisticated in their marketing, since ease of ordering had never before been a consideration. At the end of the 1950s, with younger, more dynamic men in charge, Merrythought was well placed to take on the challenges of the 'swinging sixties'.

Made in the 1940s, this 13-inch teddy is made from curly golden mohair.

1940s mohair panda bear.

1946–1948: Classic teds, Tummykins and Print Teddy

The dismal events of the decade might well have crushed a lesser company but in the 1940s Merrythought had enough grit to survive the setbacks. A small catalogue was produced in 1947, introducing a new trade name, Merrythought Verylyte, for all their products. The catalogue offered three different teddy bear ranges – the M Series, H Series and Panda Teddy – as well as an old bear favourite, Cradle Bingie, who was to be a permanent fixture in the Merrythought range until 1958 (although his name changed to Cot Bear in 1955).

'The Most Popular Of All Toy Animals' was the robust claim made on the teddy bear page of the catalogue, although whether the claim was meant to apply to all teddies or just those made by Merrythought is unclear. Of necessity, the number of size and colour options was severely restricted. The M Series, represented by an illustration used in the 1939 catalogue for the B.B. range, was described as 'The Deluxe Teddy Bear' and was made in amber-coloured long plush. Available in just three sizes – 13, 15 and 17 inches – it was kapok-filled and fitted with a squeeze growler. The following year, four options – 14, 16, 18 and 21 inches – were available. The H Series, on the other hand, had a completely new illustration which looks markedly more modern than any of Merrythought's previous traditional teddy designs. Made of golden-coloured short plush, the H Series had a fitted 'voice' and was kapok-filled, and could be 12, 15 or 17 inches tall (changing to 15, 17 and 21 inches in 1948). Panda Teddy was represented by the 1939 illustration for Panda Bear, and came in two size options, 10 or 14 inches. For the first time, sizes were also given in centimetres, an indication that Merrythought was looking for business from the export market.

Only a few pages exist for the 1948 catalogue but luckily those that survive have plenty of useful information. They reveal, for instance, that good old Bingie was back in the range where he was to remain until 1953. Panda Glove Toy was back as well, proving that the public's fascination with giant pandas had survived the war. There was also news of two exciting new teddy designs, Tummykins and Print Teddy. The blurb for Tummykins described him as 'Very soft and cuddly' and made the ambitious claim that he was 'The safest toy ever designed for little children to take to bed and snuggle up to'. He came in three sizes – 12.5, 14.5 and 16.5 inches – and was made from assorted colours of long pile plush. From examples sold at recent auctions we know that two of the colour options were black and white, and pink and white. One of Florence Attwood's most appealing non-traditional teddy designs, Tummykins remained in the Merrythought range until 1953. His fellow newcomer, however, did not fare so well. Print Teddy, 12.5 inches high, was an oddity, with a traditional mohair teddy head resting on top of body, arms and legs made 'of delightfully designed heavy quality prints'. While his cheerily patterned prints might have appealed to some, most people would have understood that with mohair still in short supply, Merrythought were making the best of the materials they had to hand. This would not have

Dating from the 1940s, this mohair panda glove puppet measures 8 inches.

This handsome, 26-inch bear made from copper-tipped mohair is believed to date from the 1940s.

17-inch black and white mohair Tummykins.

17-inch pink and white mohair Tummykins.

endeared Print Teddy to a country weary of forever having to 'make do and mend'; his appeal might have been further lessened by an inaccurate catalogue claim that he was fully jointed and fitted with a squeaker. Whether lack of sales or a change of strategy led to his departure from the range after just one brief appearance is unknown, but Print Teddy was seen no more after 1948 (although he made a brief comeback as a limited edition replica in 1996).

1949: Punkinhead

No evidence remains of a Merrythought catalogue for 1949 (perhaps because Florence Attwood's condition was worsening) but all the same the year was to see the introduction of one of the most iconic of all Merrythought bears. The 'trial book' entry for 3rd January 1949 describes the design for a young bear called Punkinhead, with the word Eaton's bracketed in the margin. Eaton's was Canada's largest department store chain and every year the Toronto store sponsored the Toronto Santa Claus Parade. This annual parade was a huge event which was entered into enthusiastically by local residents, providing very good PR for Eaton's. When Montgomery Ward, a rival department store chain, created a popular character called Rudolph the Red-Nosed Reindeer as a Christmas promotion, Eaton's hit back with an invention of their own. Their character was Punkinhead, a funny little teddy bear who had a thick woolly tuft of hair and, like Rudolph, had hurdles to overcome before he was accepted by his peers. In December 1948 Punkinhead led the Toronto Santa Claus Parade and won the hearts of thousands of children. Realising they had a merchandising gold mine on their hands, Eaton's used Punkinhead on everything from high chairs to watches, and they approached Merrythought for a soft toy version of their endearing little bear.

Although she would have been very ill when she designed him, Punkinhead

Punkinheads abound in the 'Santa's Toyland' window display, Eaton's 1953.

was arguably Florence Attwood's most significant legacy to Merrythought because as well as becoming a success in his own right, he would later be the inspiration for another bear, one whose importance to the company cannot be exaggerated. Back in January 1949, however, Punkinhead was no more than a few lines of descriptive text in the 'trial book'. The original design read as follows:

> 'Punkinhead' Young bear with Top-not of longer pile Plush than Body.
> Height 16 inches.
> Inside ears + Tummy of lighter Plush.
> Outside Ears, Head, Back Body, arms & legs of darker Plush.
> Fawn velveteen muzzle & upper foot. Felt all Paw Pads.
> Trousers Canary colour felt.
> Disced Head, arms & legs.
> Black Silk Stitched nose & mouth with corners played upwards.
> Head well rounded. Tummy well out.

This design was modified to allow for variations in the colour of the trousers, and 10 and 24-inch Punkinheads joined the 16-inch original. Further amendments appeared in the 'trial book' in 1952, including one for a Punkinhead made partially from blue and another from 'nigger brown' plush (it should be noted that the term was not recognised as offensive at the time).

Merrythought produced Punkinhead Bears for Eaton's from 1949 until 1956. There is no record of whether the arrangement was ended by mutual agreement or if one side instigated it but it is worth noting that Punkinhead designs continued to feature in the 'trial book' for several years, suggesting a continuing, amicable business relationship. The very next year, Punkinhead's close cousin Cheeky arrived on the scene at Merrythought, and unlike Punkinhead, who was exclusive to Eaton's, Cheeky could be sold in the UK and any other country Merrythought exported to, although from 1958 until 1962, Cheeky was not available in Canada. It is interesting to speculate that this might have been because Eaton's had surplus Merrythought Punkinhead stock which they wanted to sell before they would happily see a Punkinhead-inspired bear arrive on their home turf.

1950–1959: Traditional teds, Cheeky and more

For some time the safety of teddy bears and soft toys had been an area of parental concern. In the pre-war years the focus of this concern was on hygiene issues as many believed the fur and stuffing of soft toys could harbour potentially harmful germs. To counteract these worries, in the 1930s Merrythought started branding their products 'Hygienic Toys'. Other worries centred

Punkinhead was one of Florence Attwood's most successful designs.

MERRYTHOUGHT VERYLYTE Teddy Bears

THE MOST POPULAR OF ALL TOY ANIMALS

" **M** " quality is soft kapok filled and made of rich gold shaggy mohair. Unrivalled value.

" **H** " quality is soft kapok filled and made of gold medium pile mohair.

All our Bears have growlers.

The De-luxe Teddy Bear.

M / **14**, size 14″=35.5   c / m high

   / **16**,   „   16″=40.6   „   „

   / **18**,   „   18″=45.75   „   „

   / **21**,   „   21″=53.5   „   „

H / **15**, size 15″=38   c / m high

   / **17**,   „   17″=43   „   „

   / **21**,   „   21″=53.5   „   „

Sizes are approximate

All Merrythought soft Toys are filled with pure kapok, and are the lightest, softest and most cuddly of all.

Traditional teddies as offered in the 1950 catalogue.

around bears' glass eyes which were usually held in place by wire shanks or loops. One good tug was often all it took to remove the eyes, which then presented a potential choking hazard, and the sharp wire could also cause harm. Some parents took matters into their own hands by removing the glass eyes and replacing them with buttons too large to swallow easily, or by embroidering new eyes. All teddy manufacturers were aware of the eye problem and took steps to resolve it. In 1958 Merrythought started fitting all their bears with their own patent locked-in eyes which were designed to withstand even the most determined child's efforts to remove them.

15-inch golden mohair teddy from the 1950s.

With regard to design, the early years of the decade saw relatively few changes in the traditional teddy bears offered by Merrythought. The 'amber-coloured long plush' used for the M Series in the 1940s was replaced by a 'rich gold shaggy mohair' while the golden-coloured short plush of the 1940s H Series became medium pile instead. In addition, some extra sizes were gradually added, art silk options were reintroduced in 1951 and the H bears were remodelled in 1953 and again in 1954. Other than that, nothing notable changed until 1955 when the L range joined the existing M and H. Available in 9, 11, 13 and 15 inches, L range bears were 'made of best mohair London Gold plush'. This deep-piled mohair, bright verging on brassy in shade, was used again in 1956 but disappeared for a few years after that. In due course, though, it was to become the shade most closely associated with Merrythought teddy bears. In 1958 the H bear, having undergone various alterations since its first appearance in the 1931 catalogue, bowed out of the Merrythought range for good. There is little doubt its departure was hastened by the arrival of Cheeky, the design that was to dominate the company's teddy bear output for many years to come.

Cheeky's first appearance was as a 'trial book' entry for October 1955 which was headed, 'New Teddy "T." Cheeky. F & J Original'. Jean Barber was the designer at the time but the 'F&J' seems to indicate that she was tacitly acknowledging the influence of Punkinhead, a Florence Attwood design, on

Cheeky Bear, 15 inches,
dating from the late 1950s.

her new creation. The 'trial book' describes Cheeky as a 'Completely new range of bears – Tubby Teddy's (sic) – very soft stuffed with amber eyes & growls'. There is a story, which may be apocryphal, that Cheeky's name came about as a result of a member of the royal family picking him up at a trade show in 1956 and, having studied him closely, pronouncing him 'a cheeky little bear.' This story has been repeated many times, with the royal in question sometimes named as the late Queen Mother or even the present Queen; there is no hard evidence to support it but members of the royal family *did* visit the Merrythought stand at the British Industries Fair in the late 1950s so it may well be true. If so, the word 'Cheeky' above the 1955 'trial book' entry must have been added at a later date.

A young pretender with ambitions to knock the traditional teddy bear off his throne, Cheeky made his catalogue debut in 1957 on page 4, appearing opposite Merrythought's classic teddy designs. He was introduced as 'The new bear of irresistible charm. Fully jointed, kapok stuffed, bells in ears'. He was available in four different size options – 9, 11, 13 and 15 inches – and two different 'qualities'; Cheekys in the T range were made of rich gold shaggy mohair while those in the TAS range were made of thick, art-silk plush in an old gold shade. If that colour did not appeal, a further option was the PAT range which was the same as the TAS but in a variety of pastel shades. His impact was immediate, so much so that he appeared on the catalogue cover illustration the following year and remained there for years to come. In 1958

This rare Print Cheeky was a variation on Print Teddy from 1948.

the options were the same as for the previous year with the exception that a new size, 25 inches, was added, and no changes were made in 1959. The young pretender was fast on his way to becoming a modern classic.

With Cheeky satisfying the public's demand for an exciting new teddy design, Merrythought had little need to waste effort designing further new bears in the 1950s. All the same a few were created, including a new unjointed Panda Bear introduced in 1955. Made from silk plush, it came in two sizes and was described as a 'popular line' which seems to be Merrythought-speak for cheap. Popular or not, Panda Bear was gone by 1958. Pastel Bear, introduced in 1957 as either a 12 or 18-inch bear, didn't even make it into the following year's catalogue, which seems a shame as the illustration of the unjointed, soft-stuffed silk plush bear looks very appealing. He may have needed to make way for Jumpee Bear, launched in 1958 as part of a new Jumpee range of toy animals which also included a lamb, horse, rabbit and pup. Jumpee Bear measured 11 inches high and was made from 'super quality' silk plush in assorted colours. The illustration shows him having short, stumpy limbs, a poking-out tongue and little overall shape definition. To adult eyes it seems a

Front cover of the 1959 catalogue.

poor design but it must have found favour with young children (who tend to be less critical) because Jumpee Bear was back in 1959. He survived in modified form until 1967, when the Jumpees morphed into the Merry Toys range. A far more charming design, a polar bear standing on all fours, made a blink-and-you've-missed-it appearance in the 1957 catalogue. Created from white silk plush, the polar could be 9 or 15 inches long and emulated Cheeky by having bells in its ears. Another design inspired by a real animal was 1959's koala bear which came in four sizes – 6, 8, 9 and 11 inches, and was foam-stuffed and made from 'real Australian skin' according to the catalogue description. Clearly Merrythought did not want to trumpet the fact that the cute toy koala was made from the skin of dead kangaroos, hence the euphemistic 'Australian' skin. Koala Bear was to remain in the Merrythought range for most of the following decade.

Woppit: a comic book hero

One Merrythought bear from the 1950s managed to find a lasting fame that extends far beyond the realms of the specialist teddy bear collector, and did so even though it appeared in the company's range for just one year. That bear was Woppit, better known to millions as Mr Whoppit, the mascot of Donald Campbell who was famous for being the first person to hold both land and water speed records at the same time. Although the story of Mr Whoppit and Donald Campbell is fairly well known, it is worth retelling. The bear was with Campbell in his boat, Bluebird, when he broke the world water speed record on Lake Dumbleyung in Australia in 1964, achieving a speed of 276.3 mph. It was quite an adventure for a little bear, but there was much more to come. In January 1967, Campbell attempted to become the first person to do over 300 mph on water. He was attempting the record on the beautiful Coniston Water in the Lake District (Mr Whoppit was with him as usual) but things went badly wrong. While travelling at over 300 mph, Bluebird lifted out of the water and crashed back in again, disintegrating on impact. Donald Campbell's body was not found (and in fact was only recovered in 2001) but Mr Whoppit was discovered by rescuers, floating on the surface of Coniston Water. He was subsequently given to Campbell's daughter, Gina.

That much is familiar to many people, but what very few know is where the idea for Woppit came from in the first place. In fact, he was created by a prolific children's author and illustrator called Ursula Moray Williams, for a new children's comic called *Robin*. Published by Hulton Press, the company responsible for the better known *Eagle* and *Girl* comics, *Robin* was targeted at younger boys and girls. Ursula Moray Williams' *The Story of Woppit* appeared in the first issue of the comic and centred around the eponymous teddy bear

Donald Campbell's daughter Gina, with the original Mr Whoppit.

who became lost when he fell out of his owner's pram. He made friends with a donkey called Mokey and a scarecrow called Tiptop, and all three were taken in by a jolly lady called Mrs Bumble. The very simple narrative lines in *The Story of Woppit* indicate that it was intended to be read by, or to, the very young.

Hulton Press first approached Merrythought in 1953 to make toy versions of two of their other regular *Robin* characters, Richard Lion and a Siamese cat called Princess Tai-Lu, both of which duly appeared in the 1955 catalogue. Then, in September 1954, a 'trial book' entry recorded a design for 'Woppit

1. The three friends visited a farm. They made themselves very useful.

2. Tiptop scared birds off the corn. Mokey and Woppit watched him.

3. Mokey pulled the hay cart along the lane. Woppit rode on top of it.

4. Woppit drove the cows home to bed. "I am a farmer's boy!" said Woppit.

The Story of Woppit appeared in the *Robin* comic.

(*Robin* Comic)'. He was described as a 'shapeless animal, rather bear-like, tubby. Wears small coat. Brown alpaca body. Red felt coat, blue felt shoes'. The 9-inch Woppit that subsequently appeared in the 1956 catalogue was a lot more attractive than this description implies but even so he failed to make much of an impression with the toy-buying public and was gone by the following year. Nobody knows how Donald Campbell came to own a Woppit but had he not done so, it is likely that few today would remember the funny little character. Instead, thanks to his status as a brave man's mascot and the survivor of a fatal crash, he has become a teddy bear legend.

Movers and shakers: Trayton Holmes and Jimmy Matthews

Trayton Holmes, who started working at Merrythought in the late 1940s, is the man credited with establishing the company's reputation as a toy producer of the highest calibre. In John Axe's *The Magic of Merrythought*, he is quoted as saying, 'The place was all disorganised when I came to the factory and with some luck I have turned it around.' Modest modernisation was the order of the day: an automatic stuffing machine arrived in the factory and, after the premises had been purchased from the Coalbrookdale company, a programme of building and improvement was embarked on, resulting in new office space and a purpose-built showroom. Just as importantly, Holmes understood that in order to survive in the post-war economy, Merrythought needed to have a more focused approach to selling their products. To this end, one of his innovations was to exhibit at the prestigious Nuremberg trade show in 1958. Today this seems a relatively minor step to have taken but at the time it demonstrated a willingness to break into a new market that was uncharacteristic of the British toy industry in general. Traditionally, Britain ignored Europe in favour of old colonial nations such as Canada, Australia and New Zealand, but change was in the air and to his credit, Trayton Holmes recognised that. At the 1958 fair, only six British companies exhibited, and Merrythought was one of them. That Holmes had grasped the mood of the times is evidenced by the fact that just one year later, thirty British companies made the trek to Nuremberg.

It seems likely that Trayton Holmes' decision to exhibit in Europe would have been encouraged by James (Jimmy) Matthews, the Managing Director of Dean's, another British soft toy manufacturer. Matthews was a consummate salesman who understood that to create new demand for their wares, British businesses needed to get out and market them worldwide. He travelled extensively overseas for Dean's and in 1952 agreed to represent Merrythought as well. It was to prove a long-lasting association; even after his official retirement in 1976, he remained a named Director of Merrythought until 2001 when he finally resigned, aged 90. He died three years later. Jimmy Matthews is remembered with great fondness by former Merrythought staff, including designer Jacqueline Revitt. 'Over the years I built up a great friendship with Jimmy Matthews,' she told me, 'and loved and respected him to the end.'

CHAPTER FIVE

Welcome to the Sixties (1960–1969)

Getting into character

ONE OF THE MOST significant developments at Merrythought in the 1960s, at any rate as far as bears were concerned, was the development of character toys made under licence. From the very beginning the company had created toy versions of animal characters created by well known artists, starting with Chloe Preston's dog Foo-Foo in the 1931 catalogue, and an agreement with Walt Disney to make toy versions of certain Disney characters had existed since the mid-1950s. However, with the exception of Harry Rowntree's Bobby the Bear, produced in 1939, and Punkinhead, no Merrythought bear had ever originated this way. (Although the Punkinhead toy bear was made from a Florence Attwood design, the original illustrations came from artist Charles Thorsen, better known for creating Bugs Bunny.) That changed right at the very start of the 1960s, when Merrythought obtained the licence to make Sooty, Harry Corbett's phenomenally popular glove puppet bear. During the 1950s, their arch rival Chad Valley had manufactured Sooty toys and in fact many people believe that Corbett's very first teddy glove puppet had been made by Chad Valley. The story goes that when he was signed to appear on a BBC children's programme, he was told to alter the puppet's appearance to make him more memorable. Corbett's wife came up with the idea of blacking the bear's ears, and thus Sooty was born. For several years Chad Valley produced very attractive versions of Sooty made from golden mohair but by the start of the new decade, Merrythought were advertising Sooty items 'by permission Harry Corbett'.

Television played a further role in Merrythought's fortunes when a wise-cracking, anthropomorphic bear burst onto our screens. Yogi Bear first appeared in 1958 in Hanna-Barbera's *The Huckleberry Hound Show*. Audience response proved sufficiently favourable for him to star in his own programme,

18-inch Sooty nightdress case with zipped pocket.

The Yogi Bear Show, which began airing in 1961, and he was featuring in the Merrythought catalogue by 1962. A third licensed bear character first appeared in the Merrythought range in 1966 and stayed there on and off for ten years. The bear in question was Winnie the Pooh and he came to Merrythought thanks to the company's established history of making Walt Disney toys. Disney released the first of their animated Winnie the Pooh films, *Winnie the Pooh and the Honey-Tree*, in 1966 and quickly followed it in 1968 with *Winnie the Pooh and the Blustery Day*. The success of the films allowed Merrythought to develop multiple merchandising opportunities around Pooh and several of his companions.

   If creating licensed bear characters was one of Merrythought's major stories of the 1960s, another was producing bear-themed novelty items such as nightdress cases, muffs, glove puppets and so on. The company had been making nightdress cases since the 1930s but as with character toys, bears had not featured heavily until now. Finally, hand in hand with the licensed character and novelty bears came a couple of iconic character bears of Merrythought's own devising, Peter Bear and Mr & Mrs Twisty.

Design upheaval

It wasn't all change, of course. Alongside the new items, old favourites were redeveloped and experimentation continued with Cheeky, the new boy from the late 1950s. But as far as designers were concerned, the decade was very unsettled. Jean Barber left in March 1966 but even while she was still there, occasional 'trial book' entries reveal that Trayton Holmes and Jimmy Matthews were pitching in their own design ideas, some of which were credited to them alone while others acknowledged Jean Barber as a collaborative designer. Following Jean's departure, for the next few years designs came variously from Maggie Howard, Jackie Harper, Pat Baker and an individual referred to in the trial book simply as 'Durrant'. As it transpired, after Jean Barber there was to be no designer of lasting significance at Merrythought until 1972, when Jacqueline Revitt arrived. In her opinion, the problem with her immediate predecessors lay in the fact that they were not sufficiently well trained. 'It seems to me that they probably had not learned the basic disciplines of design and pattern cutting, it was after all far removed from making the odd toy, and let's face it, it's probably as much a gift as a taught science,' she believes. Towards the end of the decade, in the absence of a strong designer able to come up with ground-breaking ideas, it was just as well Merrythought had Trayton Holmes and Jimmy Matthews to steer the company through an era that was to prove notoriously tough on British soft toy manufacturers.

Marking time: Traditional teds and Cheeky

From 1960 to 1962, the only traditional teddy bear range offered by Merrythought was the M. Made from 'pure mohair pile', it was available in five sizes from 14 to 30 inches and had a fitted voice. Additionally, there was an option for the bears to be fitted with a 'Tip Growler' or music box. In fact, there was very little difference between these and earlier Merrythought bears, but that was about to change. In 1963, the M was replaced by a new range designated the NM; it too was made from mohair pile, was kapok-stuffed, had a fitted voice, and was available in five sizes (although the largest was now 32

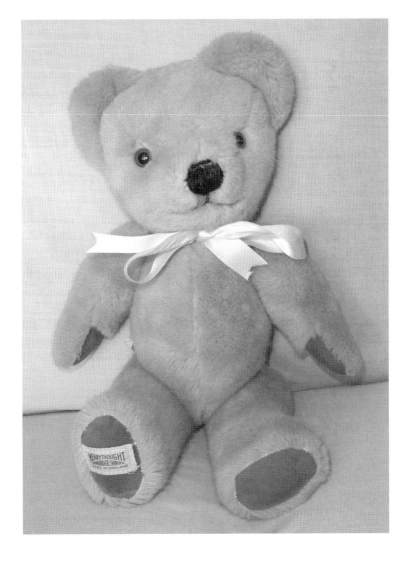

1960s golden plush bear.

Dating from the 1960s, this 15.5-inch Cheeky is made from blond mohair.

inches rather than 30). However, the similarities ended there, as this was a very different teddy bear, with a flatter face and shorter limbs which did not curve. The new Merrythought traditional teddy bear was a simpler, pared-down design with far less shape definition than anything that had gone before. Nor did the changes end there, as 1965 brought an alternative to the NM in the form of the GM which was basically the same bear in 'Super gold London pure mohair' as opposed to the rich, golden, shaggy mohair now reserved for the NM. One year later, the shaggy NM had disappeared, leaving the GM, described from 1968 as a 'Top quality traditional bear made in Old Gold Mohair plush', as Merrythought's sole standard-bearer for traditional teddy bears until the end of the decade.

If traditional teds were having a lean time, Cheeky was doing considerably better. Throughout the 1960s some new varieties were made – notably the TNY nylon plush range made in 1960 and 1961, and the short-lived O, open-mouthed range of 1962 which was also made from nylon plush – but the five size options remained unchanged. 1963 saw a return to just the T and TAS ranges, while in 1964 a new variety, the LLT, in rich London gold shaggy mohair, made an appearance but was gone within a year, replaced by the GT range made of 'Super mohair London golden plush'. In 1966 the T range vanished, leaving just the TAS and GT, and thus for Cheeky, new king of Merrythought teddy bears, the decade ended.

1960–1961: Sooty, Muff, Chimes and Miniature Bears

Sooty debuted in the Merrythought range in 1960, appearing first as a night-dress case and a 'sachet'; a sachet was actually another name for a nightie or pyjamas container although it was generally smaller than a standard night-dress case. Circular in shape, the Sooty sachet measured 12.5 inches and

Sooty in Bed nightwear
sachet.

featured Sooty's head and paws on top of a quilted 'bed' (so it looked like the famous glove puppet bear was lying in bed). It was made from 'best velveteen' with a satin pillow, and a fitted zip which opened to reveal an inner pocket in which night attire could be stored. The catalogue offered the sachet in a choice of colours – red, pink or blue. A cuddlier option was the Sooty nightdress case which measured 18 inches high and consisted of a plush Sooty head and body with a large zipped pocket. Both the sachet and nightdress case came with a magic wand attached to Sooty's paw. Over the years many wands have gone astray so it's a bonus whenever a Sooty nightdress case or sachet turns up with one intact.

A charming introduction in 1960 was the Muff Bear, part of a new range that also offered a Muff Noddy and Muff Rabbit. The catalogue declared it an 'Intriguing new novelty of our own registered designs'. Each muff had a pocket in which small hands could be kept warm, a squeaker, and a cord with which to hang the muff around a child's neck. Made from pink or blue nylon plush, the 13-inch Muff Bear featured the head of a Cheeky Bear above the muff pocket with 'arms' and 'legs' attached to it. The decision to model the muff around Cheeky rather than a traditional bear is interesting as it reflects the mood of the era which was in favour of modernity and against anything that could be perceived as 'old-fashioned'. In 1961 Muff Sooty, complete with magic wand, was added to the range and a 'trial book' entry records a Muff Punkinhead as a special order for Eaton's. By 1962, however, all the Muff Toys had vanished from the regular Merrythought line. By contrast, another item new in 1960 remained in the catalogue until the end of the decade and beyond. This was an unjointed, 4-inch bear, the design of which is attributed in the 'trial book' entry of April 1959 to 'Mr Holmes' (presumably Trayton Holmes). It is described as a 'Small sitting bear, no joints, head sewn on by hand. Ears machined in. Brown felt paw pads. Soft stuffed'. When it appeared in the 1960 catalogue, this description had been shortened to 'Small bear in hard wearing mohair plush'. The little bear remained unchanged until 1965 when it became

Pink nylon plush Muff Bear,
13 inches.

4-inch unjointed bear in blue mohair plush, designed by Trayton Holmes.

available in assorted colours. Its longevity in the catalogue is quite surprising since it is in no way a sophisticated toy, but its diminutive size might have made it popular as a mascot.

Another enduring innovation was 1961's Chime Bear which remained in production until the end of the 1960s. Measuring 9 inches high, this essentially simple design was intended as a cot toy and consisted of a teddy head on top of a cylindrical tube, with arms sewn on either side. Inside the tube, encased in wadding, was a musical chime. Made from nylon plush, Chime Bear was initially available in just the traditional baby colours of blue or pink but by 1962, when it had been joined by Chime Rabbit and Chime Cat, it came in assorted pastel colours.

1962–1964: Peter Bear and Yogi

When Merrythought unveiled an exciting new bear design in 1962, they had every reason to believe they had a new star like Punkinhead or Cheeky on their hands. Peter Bear ticked all the right boxes when it came to looks – with his large, sideways-glancing eyes, heart-shaped inset velveteen muzzle and long body that gradually separated to form two unjointed legs (his head and arms were jointed), he was decidedly modern in appearance. In fact, he still looks modern today, several decades after he was first designed. His appeal was enhanced by a smiling face and three eyelashes over each eye, while his soft, long pile mohair made him eminently huggable. It is hard to understand how he could have failed to appeal, and yet it seems that is what happened because when the 1964 catalogue was published, Peter Bear had gone. It is no secret that Peter's design was heavily influenced by a Danish comic strip called Rasmus Klump. In fact, in the 1961 'trial book' index he is referred to as 'Rasmus Klump' and his designer is given as 'Vilh. Hansen'. Rasmus Klump was the bear cub star of a popular Danish comic strip created by husband and wife team, Vilhelm and Carla Hansen in 1951. It was translated into several different languages and appeared in Britain in Glasgow's *Evening Times* as 'Bruin the Bear'. The mystery remains as to why Peter Bear's reign in the Merrythought range was so short-lived but perhaps if he had been called Bruin instead of Peter, fans of the comic strip would have identified with him and he might have had a greater chance of success. As it was, he was destined to shine briefly and then fade away until a replica was created in 2001.

Unlike Peter Bear, Yogi Bear was already familiar to millions of British householders when he arrived in the Merrythought range in 1962, thanks to the popularity of Hanna-Barbera's animated *Yogi Bear Show*. The company had obtained the rights to reproduce Yogi Bear from Screen Gems Inc., the distributor of Hanna-Barbera Productions, but they applied to the UK only. Yogi Bear's entry in the 'trial book' runs to sixteen lines of detailed description which seems excessive considering the average at that time was around eight lines, so clearly Merrythought regarded their new licensed character as important and wanted to get every detail just right. Their first Yogi Bear offerings were made in two size options, 11 inches and a 27-inch 'showpiece'. They were created from 'assorted colours in velveteen', with Yogi wearing his trademark hat, collar and tie. The following year Yogi was back as before, along with a new toy, Trike Yogi Bear, which featured a 10-inch long velveteen Yogi seated on a red pull-along tricycle. Trike Yogi proved to be a three-minute wonder and was gone by 1964, leaving the 11 and 27-inch velveteen Yogis as the only options, and one year later all traces of Yogi Bear had vanished from the catalogue. He was, however, to return for a couple of years in the early 1970s in his original format, before bowing out for good.

1965–1966: Let's do the twist

At the very start of the 1960s, a new dance phenomenon had taken the world by storm. The Twist was a rock and roll dance that originated in the USA and went on to become a global craze. While there's no evidence that the dance influenced the creation of Merrythought's next big hit, they must have known that naming their new, bendable toys 'the Twisty toys' would do them no harm whatsoever. Launched in the catalogue of 1965, the Twistys had internal flexible frames that allowed them to be manipulated into many positions; they wore simple clothes made from bright felt, and were stuffed with kapok. Initially there were four different varieties of Twisty toy – Puss, Bun, Bear and Doggie – and for each variety there was a choice of 'Mr' or 'Mrs' Twisty, presumably in an attempt to make them appeal to boys as well as girls. Mr and Mrs Twisty Bear were available in two sizes, 11 and 24 inches, and initially their heads and bodies were made from a gold coloured art silk, but by 1966,

Mr and Mrs Twisty Bear, second version.

things had changed. Now, Mr and Mrs Twisty Bear had heads made from 'best quality mohair plush', two-tone, with forehead and ears in gold and muzzles in white (the previous year their heads had been one solid colour). Their bodies and clothing had altered, too; the bodies were now made from blue suede (another rock and roll reference, although probably unintentional) and their clothes, now removable, were bright red. Mr Twisty wore the trousers and braces from the previous year with the addition of a white collar, and Mrs Twisty had been upgraded to a longer skirt with white pinafore worn over it. The size options remained unchanged.

Exciting as these changes were, the really big news was that they were joined by new additions to the Twisty clan, Mr and Mrs Twisty Cheeky (Twisty monkeys and hedgehogs were also introduced that year). The Cheeky options were available in the same sizes as the Twisty Bears, and they wore similar clothes. They remained part of the Merrythought line in 1967 and 1968 but by 1969 all that remained of the Twisty clan were Twisty Bear and Twisty Bun. They hung on until 1971 when at last the world decided it didn't want to twist any longer.

1967–1969: The dominance of Pooh

For Merrythought, the big story of 1967 was the dominance of Disney's Winnie the Pooh and chums. In 1966 the first Pooh toy had appeared, wearing a bright red top emblazoned with his name, and accompanied by Kanga and Roo, Eeyore and Piglet. By 1967 the company had obtained the licensing rights for a great swathe of global territory comprising Great Britain, Canada, the Near, Middle and Far East, Australia, Sweden, 'British' West Indies, Bahamas and Bermuda, and now it intended to make the most of this golden opportunity. The very first page of the 1967 catalogue introduced the new Walt Disney lines including 9-inch Chime versions of Pooh, Kanga,

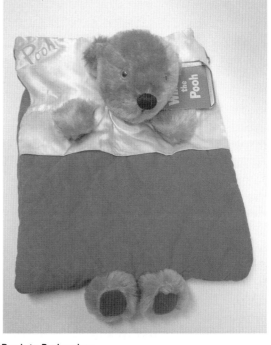

Pooh in Bed sachet.

Merrythought Pooh
Bear without the
original red top.

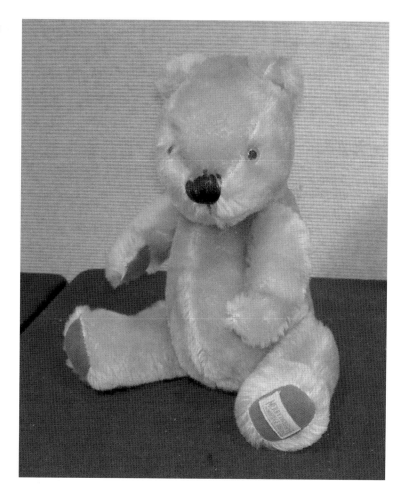

Wol and Piglet. On the next page the 10 and 24-inch Winnie the Poohs from
the previous year were back again, made from 'hard wearing mohair plush'
and jointed at head and arms. Similarly handsome versions of Piglet, Tigger,
Kanga, Roo, Wol, Rabbit and Eeyore were also listed on this page. Further into
the catalogue, in keeping with the era's fondness for bed clothes receptacles,
two Pooh nightdress cases were offered. 'Pooh in Bed' featured a Pooh made
of brown mohair plush, lying in a quilted velveteen and satin bed beneath
which there was a zipped pocket. Meanwhile, in the 'Super range of nightdress cases', there was a fine-looking, 21-inch Pooh nightie case made from
best quality mohair plush. One year later, everything was the same except that
Chime Pooh had gone, and then in 1969 the big Pooh nightdress case disappeared. The Pooh in Bed sachet remained in the range until 1973 and then
departed, as did the 10 and 24-inch mohair Winnie the Pooh character toys
but they, unlike Pooh in Bed, returned for a brief moment of glory in 1976.

9-inch Chime Pooh.

The Fisher Price years

In 1967, Merrythought became sole concessionaires in the UK for Fisher Price
Toys. Founded in 1930, by coincidence the exact same year as Merrythought,
the American company originally made toys from pine and steel with colour

lithographs adding charm. Brightly coloured plastic toys were introduced in the 1950s and by the late 1960s their classic toys such as the 'Melody Push Chime' and 'Cackling Hen' were familiar to children throughout Britain.

It was a sensible arrangement for Merrythought as Fisher Price Toys complemented rather than competed with their own products, but it was to prove all too short-lived; the last catalogue declaring Merrythought sole concessionaire for Fisher Price was published in 1971. The reason for the change is unknown but Fisher Price was taken over by The Quaker Oats Company in 1969 and that might have had some bearing on the matter.

CHAPTER SIX

Bridging Troubled Waters (1970–1989)

Teddy in jeopardy

AT THE START of the 1970s, the British soft toy industry was in dire straits. The previous decade had seen the demise of several major names including Chiltern, J.K. Farnell and Wendy Boston, and even the seemingly invincible Chad Valley had begun the decline that would result in it being taken over by Palitoy in the late 1970s. For the companies that remained, the going was getting very tough indeed. This downturn in fortunes is usually blamed on fierce competition from Far Eastern imports, which were cheaper than British-made products because of lower labour costs. This is true but it tells just part of the story; while there is no denying that cheap imports played a big part in reducing the demand for British soft toys, the market was also hit by a gradual shift away from traditional toys such as teddy bears, a shift that history has tended to attribute to a change in children's tastes. Whether this is an accurate reading of the situation is debatable. When I was growing up in the 1960s, my teddy bear was very important to me as a reassuring bedtime companion (and occasional playmate), and I know my sisters and school friends were likewise attached to their bears. Unlike today's children who own multiple soft toys, we tended to have just one teddy to whom we confided our secrets and fears. Rather than children falling out of love with the teddy bear, I believe it was their parents (the adults ultimately responsible for deciding which toys to buy) who failed to keep faith with it. This was an era during which everything was changing – the Empire was melting away as former British colonies gained their independence, metric measurements took over from the old imperial ones, decimalisation loomed, and technology advanced so rapidly that the Americans were able to put men on the moon at the end of the decade. With so much change afoot, many parents must have felt their children needed toys that reflected the mood of the times instead of those that were perceived, however misguidedly, as old-fashioned and unexciting.

So, the situation at the start of the 1970s was that there was less demand for teddy bears and much of the demand that did exist was being met by cheap imports. It also didn't help that the typical teddy bear of the time was a fairly dismal creation, unjointed and made of synthetic materials which very often came in garish colours. Except, that is, at Merrythought, where they bucked the trend and continued to create high quality, traditionally-styled teddy bears whilst occasionally experimenting with more innovative designs. Ironically for a company that has earned criticism in recent years for failing to keep up with the times, this strategy of looking to the past proved exactly the right thing to do. Although smaller than it had once been, a market neverthe-less remained for traditional teddy bears and Merrythought was one of a very few companies able to supply it. By catering to this niche market for classic teddies while continuing to produce a good variety of other well-made soft toys, Merrythought managed to stay on solid ground at a time when other toy companies were losing their footing and going under.

19-inch London Gold mohair teddy, 1970s, complete with original swing label.

Decline and renaissance: Cheeky and classic teds

Throughout the 1970s, Merrythought continued to offer versions of Cheeky made from golden mohair (London Gold from 1974 to 1981) and also from different types of synthetic plush including 'Super thick Dark Mink plush', 'Simulated Mink' and 'Brown Dreylon'. The mohair ranges were available in six sizes ranging from 9 to 25 inches, as was the Dark Mink plush range, made in 1970 for one year only, and the Brown Dreylon which featured in 1974 and 1975. There were fewer options – 15, 18 and 25 inches – for the Simulated Mink range which ran from 1971 for ten years. Then in the 1980s something rather

This 25-inch Cheeky dates from the 1970s and is made from synthetic plush.

odd happened. The first half of the decade saw a flurry of activity as new colours such as pink, blue and champagne were introduced to the plush range, and size options were slashed across the board. By 1985 there were just four Cheeky offerings in the catalogue, all measuring 12 inches and available in London Gold, Champagne, Blue and Pink. One year later even this reduced choice had gone, and Cheeky – former young pretender to the Merrythought crown, latterly undisputed king of the teddy bears – had vanished completely. Although still available by special order, he would not be seen again as a mainstream product for several years.

At the same time that Cheeky was declining, Merrythought's more traditional teds were enjoying something of a renaissance. Of course the 'traditional' teddies now bore little resemblance to the pre-war bears. Faces were flatter, muzzles were unshaven, limbs were shorter and they had much less shape definition than before. Gone were the trademark webbed claws and any hint of a hump at the back, but despite all these changes, the quality of the mohair remained consistently high. Following its brief appearance in the mid-1960s, London Gold reappeared in 1974 as the default colour for traditional teddies and it remains so to this day. The 1970s also offered a range of classic-style bears made in Simulated Mink and Brown Dreylon. From 1971 onwards, the

Mint condition, 9-inch golden mohair Cheeky from the 1970s, complete with original Merrythought and Made in Great Britain swing labels.

1970s simulated mink Cheeky, 15 inches.

Having starred on catalogue covers in the 1970s, by the mid-1980s Cheeky had (temporarily) gone from hero to zero.

size options for both the mohair and synthetic plush bears went up to a massive 48 inches, the largest a Merrythought teddy bear had ever been. It's hard to tidy away a 4ft teddy bear so presumably these big boys were intended to be permanently on display. It is tempting to read this as an indication of things to come, since before too long teddies were going to wander across the boundary that separates playthings and collectables, and become objects of desire for adults as well as children.

The 1980s saw quite a few new arrivals in the traditional bear range, none of which stayed for very long. The S-Series of Aristocrat Bears which featured in 1983 and 1984 harked back to earlier designs with their shaved muzzles and distinctive noses featuring dropped vertical stitches at either side. These attractive bears were made from synthetic plush in a shade described as cinnamon, although it was actually much lighter than the term suggests. Another striking but short-lived introduction was the Ironbridge grey bear made from 'pure mohair'; it debuted in 1985 and was gone by the following year. Other synthetic plush colour options of the mid-1980s included Champagne and Nutmeg, as well as the more traditional London Gold. Again, this colour experimentation was indicative of a subtle shift towards making bears for a changing

Pink plush Cheeky dating from the 1980s.

Although charming in their own right, 1970s 'traditional' Merrythought teddies like this 10-inch example, made from London Gold mohair, were far removed from the company's earliest teddy offerings.

market, as was the introduction, in 1987, of a 5-inch miniature bear made from London Gold mohair. It came boxed and was therefore very suitable as a souvenir or gift.

Bears in uniform

The earliest years of the 1970s brought little innovation in teddy bear design, although a 1971 range of 'Sticky Toys' which had arms and legs that could stick to other parts of the toy's body included a Sticky Bear. This had a white

Beefeater Bear,
introduced in 1973.

nylon plush head that looked vaguely Cheeky-ish, and a soft stuffed nylon body which came in various bright colours. The range failed to make an impact and had disappeared by the following year. More successful was the re-emergence of the Muff Bear in a redesigned format, and Yogi Bear who made a comeback that lasted from 1971 to 1973. However, during the first part of the decade the big story was the arrival of a series of uniformed bears, the design of which clearly owed a lot to the dressed Bingies of the 1930s. Unlike the Bingies, however, these bears were unjointed. When they burst onto the scene in 1972 there were just two of them – London Guardsman and London Policeman – but by the following year this initial pair had been joined by Highlander and Beefeater Bear. They had heads, 'hands and feet' (to use Merrythought's terminology) made from mohair, and bodies dressed in appropriate uniforms. The Guardsman, who was available in 21 and 30-inch size options, wore a bright red uniform with an imitation thick pile bearskin while the Policeman could be 20 or 28 inches and wore a black uniform with classic policeman's helmet. Beefeater Bear and Highlander Bear, both introduced in 1973, were available in 18 or 25-inch size options; the Beefeater was dressed in a smart red coat and trousers bordered with yellow and black braid, and Highlander Bear wore a bright tartan kilt with a white sporran, and a tartan tam o'shanter. Due to his short kilt Highlander Bear, unlike his fellows, had legs made of mohair. All four uniformed bears made it into the 1974 catalogue but by 1975 only Guardsman and Beefeater remained, and they too had gone by 1976. However, their day was not yet done as they all re-emerged in 1986 with the exception of the Policeman, who duly joined them one year later. The size options had now altered so that they all came in a choice of three sizes: 18 inches, 36 inches and a whopping 78 inches. These outsized bears were often bought by toy or gift shops in popular tourist locations because when placed on the pavement outside the shop, they couldn't fail to attract attention. When Policeman Bear made his comeback in 1987 he brought along an all new design, Traffic Warden Bear, who proved to be about as popular as the human variety and bombed out of the range after just one year. The other four hung on together until the end of the decade when they were redesigned in synthetic plush and were gradually joined by a whole cast of new characters, including a Chelsea Pensioner and Fighter Pilot. They were now known collectively as the Heritage Collection.

Flexi Bears, Cuddle-Cubs, Tickle Tummies and more

While Merrythought's awareness of the growing adult market influenced the introduction of the uniformed bears, and even to some extent the redevelopment of their traditional teddies, they nevertheless kept a keen interest in the bedrock of their business, the children's market. In this sector cuddly night-

Guardsman and Policeman Bears from the 1973 catalogue.

dress cases made in the shape of teddies, pandas, polar bears and even koalas, continued to be important throughout the 1970s and 1980s. Alongside the nightdress cases, attempts were made to come up with toys that could be played with rather than just hugged and loved. The short-lived Sticky Toys of 1971 fell into this category, as did an equally short-lived Flexi Boy and Girl Bear, part of a range introduced in 1975 that included Flexi Puss and Flexi Rabbit. Hailed by Merrythought as 'An outstanding concept in soft toys', the Flexi range featured toys which were fitted with wire frames to allow them to be placed in different positions. The claim that they created 'an endless variety of positions for outstanding play value' seems not to have impressed the public because the Flexi Boy and Girl Bear were gone by 1976 and the entire range had disappeared one year later.

By contrast, the Floppy toy range, which included a panda when introduced in 1975, offered no ground-breaking play concept, just an ultra-soft, reasonably lifelike animal toy which children could hug and love. Perhaps because it did not try to be too clever, the Floppy range proved more enduring than the Sticky or Flexi Toys, remaining in the catalogue until 1981, although the panda was replaced by a polar bear from 1976 onwards. It seems that what Merrythought did well around this time was make attractive, cuddly toys with which children could choose to invent games of their own devising, or simply hug for comfort. Another range that fulfilled this brief was the Softies, introduced in 1985 with bear, panda and polar versions, although it proved less successful than the Floppy range and did not reappear in 1986. Instead, in 1987 yet another new range was launched, this time combining the soft cuddly appeal of the Floppies and Softies with some of the poseability of the Sticky and Flexi Toys. Cuddle-Cubs, the catalogue blurb declared, 'are super soft and specially constructed to adopt many fun positions without the use of wires or stiffeners'. From the very start bears figured heavily in the line; there were Honey Bear, Polar Bear, Brown Bear and Panda Bear Cuddle-Cubs, all available in a choice of two sizes, 16 and 24 inches. The Cuddle-Cubs lasted with some variations until the end of the 1980s and then reappeared in slightly altered form in the early 1990s. Another new line, the Tickle Tummies, appeared in 1989, featuring, amongst several different animal designs, a panda and an unspecified bear. At 10 inches, they were unjointed and softly stuffed, and were made in a seated position which exposed their softly inviting tummies, hence the name 'Tickle Tummies'. An innovative feature of these toys, which continued to be made into the early 1990s, was the claw and pad definition picked out on their 'hands' and 'feet'.

In addition to the ranges highlighted in this chapter, a large number of 'real' (as opposed to 'teddy') bear designs came and went throughout the 1970s and 1980s. Various panda, polar and koala toys all appeared regularly in the Merrythought catalogue and their continued presence vouches for their popularity with children. By 1989, however, it was clear that change was in the air at Ironbridge, a change that would ultimately render children's likes and dislikes far less important than they had once been. The company had already been experimenting with limited edition bears but what they had been making was small fry compared to the deluge of collectors' bears the 1990s would bring. With hindsight, a minor entry in the 1989 catalogue seems an augury of things to come. In amongst pages showing a selection of classically-inspired teddy bears, uniformed bears and children's offerings such as the Tickle Tummies, there appeared a novelty item which took the form of a 26-inch Christmas stocking with a small-ish Merrythought bear tucked into a side pocket. Redolent with nostalgia, summoning as it did rosy images of perfect Christmas mornings, this item was intended to appeal to adults as much as to children. Although it appeared without any fanfare, sharing a page towards the back of the catalogue with gollies, a clown toy and sundry other items, the Xmas Stocking with Bear nevertheless heralded the age of the collectors' bear at Merrythought.

Unjointed panda,
circa 1980.

SUPPLEMENTARY LINES TO THE 1989 RANGE

MERRYTHOUGHT

The leading Soft Toy Manufacturer *Est.1930*

Complimentary to the 1989 Brochure

BRITISH INTERNATIONAL TOY FAIR
LONDON · 28 JANUARY 1989

G19/1S "Su-Lin" Siamese Cat *Size 18"*	£15.95
G19/1B "Lucky" Black & White Cat *Size 18"*	£15.95
G19/1G "Mimi" Smokey Grey Cat *Size 18"*	£15.95

G16/1 "Chi-an" Panda Bear *Size 18"*	£29.50
G16/4 "Chi-an" Panda Bear *Size 44"*	£137.50

G17/1 "Danny" Donkey *Size 24"*	£29.50
G17/6 "Danny" Donkey *Size 72"*	£995.00

G18/1 "Benson" Bear *Size 20"*	£29.50
(Showpiece also available).	

Merrythought SOFT TOYS

MERRYTHOUGHT LIMITED
IRONBRIDGE · TELFORD · SHROPSHIRE · TF8 7NJ
TEL 0952 45 3116 · FAX 0952 45 2054 · TELEX 35438 Telcom G

CONFORMS TO B.S. 5665 · MADE IN ENGLAND

1989 catalogue supplement showing two 'real' bear designs.

New faces: Oliver Holmes and Jacqueline Revitt

In 1972, two individuals who were to play hugely significant roles in Merrythought's future arrived on the scene. The first, Oliver Holmes, was 22 when he joined Merrythought. For some time he worked alongside his father at Merrythought but when ill health forced Trayton to step down, Oliver took over. To him fell the difficult job of steering Merrythought through turbulent times as radical changes in the teddy bear and soft toy market forced the company to rethink its strategy in ways that would have been incomprehensible to its founding fathers.

Although he has devoted his working life to Merrythought, at heart Oliver Holmes is something of a 'boy's own' adventurer who has piloted hot-air balloons and recently took part in the centenary re-run of the Peking-to-Paris motor car rally. In partnership with his childhood friend Malcolm Corrie, he completed the gruelling race in a vehicle originally constructed in the 1920s for the New York Fire Department. The pair encountered some fairly hair-raising experiences during the six weeks it took to complete the rally but it was worth the effort as by the time they reached the finish line in Paris, they

Merrythought Christmas staff lunch, 1972; far left is Trayton Holmes, next to him is Jacqueline Revitt and standing third from the right is Oliver Holmes.

had raised approaching £10,000 for Ataxia UK, a charity that funds medical research into a rare genetic disorder called Friedreich's Ataxia.

The second important new arrival in 1972 was Jacqueline Revitt, a trained couture tailoress and dressmaker who was employed by Trayton Holmes as a soft toy designer. As she discovered right from the start, there was to be no easing in to the position for her. 'I saw Harrods buyers on my first day!' she recalls. The job required Jacqueline to meet with clients and discuss a new range of toys for the coming season. 'I then had to produce prototypes for their approval. The first item I designed was a baby seal and as far as I know it is still available. I also produced a range of new items for the toy fairs including a show-stopping piece for the

Oliver Holmes (left) and Malcolm Corrie before the start of the Peking-to-Paris rally.

London show. This usually found its way into Harrods as their centrepiece for the next Christmas season, and of course I designed a whole range of toys for the annual catalogue.' As a key member of staff, Jacqueline reported solely to Trayton Holmes (except when Sales Director Jimmy Matthews visited to discuss new ranges). She found him a very considerate employer. 'Without doubt I worshipped Trayton Holmes,' she recalls, 'in many ways he was like a father to me – very wise, great fun, very fair and he was very kind to me, quickly identifying if I felt awkward and looking after me. And he understood that as an artist you simply couldn't churn out design after design to order; he often advised me to go for a walk along the river. (I never did, there were those who would not approve.) I still miss those twinkling mischievous eyes and I still miss him greatly.'

Jacqueline's recollections of her early days at Merrythought help paint a picture of what life was like there in the 1970s. 'The atmosphere was very strict in some areas, mixing with the factory staff was frowned on but I made it very clear that I was not a devotee of class distinction and I made many lasting friends with the factory girls, most of whom were very willing to help. Having said it was strict, we still had so much fun and it was a very happy place to work.'

After five years at Merrythought, Jacqueline became seriously unwell and required surgery followed by a period of convalescence. She was asked to resign by Oliver Holmes but rejoined the company at his invitation in 1983 and was eventually made Design Director. The new responsibilities allowed her to make full use of her creativity. 'I loved being able to develop exciting new mohairs with lovely unusual finishes,' she remembers. 'Merrythought were allowed to have these new mohairs exclusively for a year; this gave us the edge and we produced some very fine bears as the bears were now the big news in the soft toy business.'

It wasn't long before Jacqueline's clever designs started earning plaudits and awards for Merrythought. 'My first award was quite soon after I started when, at the British Toy and Hobby Fair, a range of realistic floppy animals won an award for unique design and styling. Oliver had a copy of the award made for my office and I was absolutely delighted. I then went on to win the prestigious TOBY (Teddy Bear of the Year) award for Master Mischief. It was the first bear to tell a story and it is the one I am most proud of. I dedicated it to my mother who always said "One day you will be famous", and I suppose for one brief moment I was. Paleface won another TOBY and several others won various awards, some in Holland, Canada and the States. I wish I could remember them all.'

It is Jacqueline's opinion, and one with which legions of collectors would concur, that aside from winning the awards, her greatest achievement was having the vision to see there was a lot more mileage in Jean Barber's Cheeky. 'I changed a few pieces and colours and made him into a Guardsman. Also, making him so tiny was a real winner, this breathed new life into a superb design which had sadly fallen by the wayside but the new little characters put him into the collector market and brought him to the attention of the American and Japanese collectors. Thank goodness; Merrythought sold little else in the latter years.'

CHAPTER SEVEN

The Age of the Collector
(1990–2005)

———◇———

Display, not play

SOMETIME IN THE early 1980s, a trend that had materialised originally in
the US made its way across the Atlantic and began, slowly at first, to take hold
in the UK. The trend was for adults to own – and openly discuss owning –
teddy bears, items which until now had been regarded, by and large, as strictly
for children. In fact, as it turned out, a great many people felt enormous affection for teddy bears but kept silent about it in the belief that they were alone,
and that to admit to liking teddies was somehow shameful. Then towards the
tail end of the 1960s, along came Peter Bull, a British actor and ardent teddy
bear enthusiast, who confessed to his passion for teddies on a widely watched
American television programme. He was promptly deluged with letters from
fellow arctophiles and was even sent teddies by people who wanted their
childhood companion to go to a good home. A book followed, and Peter Bull
stepped into the annals of teddy bear history. Suddenly, in America at least,
the genie was out of the bottle as sane, respectable individuals started talking
openly about their love for teddy bears. As interest spread, people began to
scour thrift shops and junk stalls in search of vintage teddy bears (which could
be bought for next to nothing at the time). In due course, astute companies
and craft-workers became aware of the potential presented by this surge of
interest in old bears. Not everyone, they reasoned, would want to bring an
old, tatty and possibly bug-infested teddy bear into their homes, so they began
creating heirloom-type teddies for fastidious arctophiles.

During the 1980s this teddy bear renaissance gathered momentum and
spread across the US but it was slow to catch on in the UK. However, little by
little, word was spreading and an increasing number of respectable adults
gradually started to step out of the teddy bear closet. A major step was taken

in 1985 when Ian Pout transformed his antiques-cum-gift shop into Teddy Bears of Witney, the first UK shop dedicated to selling old and new teddy bears. By now, soft toy manufacturers had cottoned on to the demand for adult-friendly teddy bears and had started to produce handsome, tradition- ally styled bears that were intended for display, not play. Other dedicated teddy bear shops began to appear and wherever they sprang up, new arctophiles were born. At last, as the 1980s came to an end, the stage was set for Britain to go all-out bear crazy.

Merrythought and Tide-Rider Inc.

As teddy mania swept the US in the early 1980s, Tide-Rider, Merrythought's California-based American distributor, identified the possibilities presented by the trend and decided to take action. Merrythought was asked to come up with a traditional teddy bear design which would appeal to an adult market and could be sold as a limited edition. The result of that first request was the Edwardian, a fully jointed mohair bear with some of the features commonly associated with early teddies including a shaved muzzle, webbed claw stitching and long, curving arms. Three different versions of the Edwardian were made but only one, the 18-inch bear made from a lovely long pile English mohair, was a limited edition. Produced in an edition of 1,000, it came boxed and had a label signed by Trayton Holmes (who was still Merrythought's Chairman at the time). When it went on sale in the US, the Edwardian was an immediate success, especially the limited edition which sold out completely. As far as the American market was concerned, the writing on the wall was clear: limited editions were the way to go. Soon after the Edwardian, Jacqueline Revitt designed a set of bears depicting the four seasons, each one made from a different coloured short-pile mohair; Spring was white, Summer beige, Autumn brown and Winter grey. To link the bears to their seasons, each one wore clothing appropriate to the time of year; Spring, for example, wore a pretty frock and carried a basket of spring flowers while Winter wore a red waistcoat, a Father Christmas hat and carried a bell. Again limited to 1,000 pieces, the Seasonal Bear Collection was another big success.

As time progressed, Merrythought produced an increasingly inventive selection of bears for their lucrative American market. Tide-Rider's associa- tion with Merrythought was proving beneficial and relations between Jacqueline Revitt and Tide-Rider's Linda Smith became very friendly. 'Oliver Holmes gave me the opportunity to travel abroad, for which I am eternally grateful,' she recalls. 'To my joy I met Linda Smith and her son David who were Merrythought's distributors in the States. I am proud to say that we established a lasting friendship and have vacationed with them many times.' By the start of the 1990s, however, the UK was fast catching up with the US in

Tide-Rider's Linda Smith reviewing her exclusive range of Merrythought bears.

its demand for collectable teddy bears, so Merrythought began to explore the new possibilities offered by its home market.

Limited Edition bears

In 1980 Merrythought had been in existence for fifty years but apart from a reference on the front of that year's catalogue, Golden Jubilee celebrations appear to have been low-key, to the point of non-existent. Ten years later, however, things were very different and the company's Diamond Jubilee was treated as an event of real significance. To mark the occasion, a special Diamond Jubilee Bear was created; measuring 18 inches and made from blond

Jacqueline Revitt
holding the
prototype Diamond
Jubilee Bear, 1990.

mohair, it featured a woven Merrythought Jubilee logo on its right paw and came in a smart blue presentation box tied with blue ribbon. The Diamond Jubilee Bear was made in a worldwide limited edition of 2,500, a huge number which these days only a supremely confident manufacturer would commit to, but in the halcyon early days of collectable teddy bears, the demand more than justified the edition size and the bear sold out swiftly.

The success of the Diamond Jubilee Bear gave Merrythought food for thought, as did the increasing number of requests they were receiving from UK arctophiles envious of the imaginative collectors' bears they knew Merrythought was making exclusively for the American market. Why, the British collectors asked, were these bears not available on home ground? It was a good question, and one to which Merrythought paid close attention. In 1991, in addition to the usual annual catalogue containing details of the latest toy ranges, a new catalogue, the Merrythought International Collectors'

Catalogue, was introduced and as its name implies, it was aimed squarely at the collectors' market. The majority of the featured bears were made from mohair and came in limited editions of varying sizes. There were all-new designs in the catalogue, as well as those that looked to the past for inspiration. Chief amongst these was a replica of an old friend from the 1930s, the Magnet Bear. (A rather spectacular version of this bear, made from a vibrant-coloured mohair described as amethyst, was to appear in 1999, in advance of the millennium celebrations, as a limited edition of 2000.)

Once the floodgates had been opened, there was to be no going back. Merrythought continued to make superb quality soft toys for the children's

Millennium Magnet from 1999, Ltd Ed 90/2000.

In 1992 a limited edition Mr Whoppit replica was produced.

market but at the same time they stepped up their commitment to creating bears for collectors. In the International Collectors' Catalogue of 1992, a groundbreaking bear designed by Jacqueline Revitt, now Merrythought's Design Director, won the company universal acclaim. Master Mischief was a 14-inch golden mohair bear dressed in short, patched dungarees, holding a catapult behind his back. The overall effect of a little boy feigning innocence over some wrong-doing was extremely appealing and the TOBY award it won was well-deserved. 1992 also saw the arrival of a limited edition Mr Whoppit, created from the same pattern as the 1956 Woppit. Now famous as Donald Campbell's mascot bear, the 9-inch Mr Whoppit was made in a massive edition of 5,000 and, like the Diamond Jubilee Bear, was presented in a smart box with double-fronted opening. The following year, a couple of important anniversaries provided the inspiration for two memorable bears in the International Collectors' Catalogue. One of these, the Mount Everest Bear, commemorated the 50th anniversary of the conquest of Everest. Made in a limited edition of 5,000, it

Sixty-one years after Rupert's name first appeared in the 'trial book', Merrythought finally issued their first Rupert Bear.

came in an attractive presentation box which bore a facsimile of Sir Edmund Hillary's autograph. The second anniversary bear of 1993 marked forty years since the coronation of Queen Elizabeth II. Made as a limited edition of 5,000, it was made from red, white and blue mohair as befitted a bear made to celebrate such a patriotic occasion. Again, like the Everest Bear, it came in a smart presentation box. Itself a reworking of an idea that originated in 1953, the Coronation Bear was redesigned in time for the 50th anniversary of

Issued in 1993, this striking red, white and blue bear marked the 40th anniversary of the Queen's coronation.

the Queen's coronation in 2003. Another significant arrival in 1993 was an appropriately dressed Rupert Bear, which could be bought in a standard 18 inches or ordered specially at 78 inches. The first Merrythought Rupert to appear since that tantalising 1932 'trial book' entry (see Chapter 3), it remained in production for eight years.

Throughout the 1990s and into the new millennium, the collectors' catalogues continued to offer a satisfying mix of innovative new designs, replicas raided from the archives, and commemorative bears marking everything from the death of Princess Diana to the 150th anniversary of the birth of suffragette heroine Emmeline Pankhurst. In addition to their catalogue items, a new market opened up for Merrythought as more and more specialist teddy bear

Master Mischief won Jacqueline Revitt a TOBY award.

Mount Everest Bear celebrated the 50th anniversary of the conquering of Everest.

retailers sprang up across the country. These shops frequently requested 'shop exclusives' which were unavailable anywhere else. Foremost amongst these shops was Teddy Bears of Witney which championed Merrythought from the very beginning, but many others also played their part. Collectors were made aware of the shop exclusives – as well as the regular collectors' catalogue items – by the very popular specialist teddy bear magazines which were published monthly and could be purchased from W.H. Smith's and other large newsagents, as well as by subscription. The importance of these magazines in popularising the teddy bear hobby cannot be overstated. In Britain there were three titles, *Teddy Bear Scene*, *Teddy Bear Times* and *Teddy Bear Club International* – one or all of which were bought by the majority of British arctophiles. The US offered *Teddy Bear and Friends* and *Teddy Bear Review*. Several European countries also produced their own magazines, as did Australia and South Africa, presenting manufacturers like Merrythought with an enormous potential marketplace.

Another new market for limited edition bears came via specialist mail order

Publications like *Teddy Bear Scene* brought Merrythought's products to the attention of a worldwide marketplace.

collectable companies such as Compton & Woodhouse and Lawleys by Post, both of which commissioned a number of Merrythought bears. These would be widely advertised in national newspapers and magazines, thereby introducing Merrythought products to an audience far beyond its usual niche market. Thus, as well as earning the company vital revenue, these ventures also offered Merrythought the opportunity to convert those with no more than a casual interest in bears into dedicated Merrythought collectors.

Return of the king: Cheeky makes a comeback

In the first International Collectors' Catalogue (published in 1991), an old friend who had been absent from the Merrythought range since 1986 made a welcome comeback. Cheeky, Merrythought's golden boy of the 1950s, 1960s

A limited edition
Cheeky made
exclusively for Teddy
Bears of Witney.

and 1970s, had been available only as a special order since disappearing from the catalogue but now, thanks to demand from collectors at home, in the US and in Japan (where Cheeky holds iconic status), he was back. Jacqueline Revitt took the basic Cheeky design and reinvented him over and over again, producing him in different sizes, materials, colours and costumes, including the popular 6-inch Micro Cheeky introduced in 1994 and the later Cheeky Punkie, a sort of Cheeky/Punkinhead hybrid which was well received by

When Cheeky emerged from out of the wilderness, he was produced in a wide selection of colours and styles.

This limited edition 'Mr & Mrs Twisty Cheeky Punkie' ingeniously incorporated three separate classic Merrythought designs into one.

collectors. Thanks to the endless makeovers, Cheeky became the ultimate master of disguise and it's probably fair to say that even when interest in Merrythought's other limited edition bears fell away during the early years of the new millennium, Cheeky's popularity kept the company ticking over. As with the non-Cheeky designs, dozens of exclusives were made for specialist retailers anxious to meet their customers' seemingly insatiable appetite for all things Cheeky. After a period in the wilderness, the young pretender had come of age and had returned to claim his crown.

Joining the club: Merrythought International Collectors' Club

As collecting limited edition bears became an established hobby, manufacturers started to look for new ways to capitalise on the trend and secure the
loyalty of their collectors. In 1992, Steiff pioneered the idea of a collectors' club
which offered many benefits including the opportunity to purchase exclusive
members-only bears. Other manufacturers soon followed suit, with British
firm Dean's launching their own club in 1994 and Merrythought following
suit with the Merrythought International Collectors' Club in 1995. In return
for a modest fee, members received various benefits including a silver wishbone lapel pin, a quarterly newsletter and the opportunity to purchase
exclusive Club bears. It's difficult to gauge exactly how many members the
Club had at its peak, but a magazine article of 1997 quotes 1,300, while
according to former Club Secretary Peter Andrews, there were around 600
members in 2002. This contrasts with the claim of around 2,000 club members
made by Oliver Holmes in a *Daily Mail* article in December 2006. Since the
article was reporting on the recent closure of Merrythought, it is strange that
the Club membership at the time was more than three times the 2002 figure.
However, a possible explanation for this apparent incongruity is that a year
or so before the company's closure, membership fees were abolished, as were
some of the benefits including the silver wishbone pin. Since joining was now
free, it is entirely possible that many new bear enthusiasts signed up. In some
ways the move was clever as it brought the Club exclusives to the attention of

Blenheim and
Chatsworth, 2nd and
3rd Merrythought
International
Collectors' Club
teddy bears.

a wider audience and thus increased the chance of sales, but some existing Club members regretted the change as they felt it devalued the significance of membership.

Open Days

When membership of the Merrythought International Collectors' Club was made free, one of the benefits that existing members lost was a complimentary invitation to the annual Open Day. Introduced in 1996, this annual beano swiftly became an eagerly anticipated event for most Club members because of the opportunity it gave them for mixing with fellow enthusiasts whilst enjoying Merrythought's rather lavish hospitality. So popular was it that in 1997, an estimated 1,000 people attended the event. Held at the factory premises and nearby Dale End Park, an attractive piece of parkland on the banks of the River Severn, the Open Day offered a host of activities designed to entertain arctophiles and their families. Themed along the lines of a traditional summer fete, it was usually opened by a civic dignitary or celebrity, and there was always a huge marquee filled with attractions such as a silent auction, best-dressed bear competition, tombola, exhibits of vintage Merrythought bears, large-scale display toys and lots more. Outside the marquee, various sideshows offered chances to win Merrythought toys, musical entertainers kept the atmosphere lively and some years there were even free boat trips on the Severn. All this was enormous fun but for dedicated collectors, the first port of call was to the factory premises to acquire the latest Open Day bear and then rummage like mad for bargains amongst the factory seconds. Very often there was nothing wrong with these items and they were simply being sold off cheaply because their sales figures had been low or space was needed for newer items. It was also possible to tour the factory to watch the various skilled workers ply their trade – stuffing, fixing eyes, stitching noses etc – and sometimes there was the chance to have a part-made bear finished to individual specifications.

  While the factory visit was important to the serious collectors, for many visitors the highlight of the day was the moment when the buffet tent opened. This was the signal for hoards of hungry Club members to descend on the tent and line up in front of tables groaning with food. There was nothing sophisticated about the fare – sausage rolls, chicken pieces and sandwiches were standard – but there was plenty of it and judging by the towering piles of food seen on many plates, it was very much appreciated. I recall Merrythought Open Days as happy, charmingly anachronistic occasions which showed the company at its best. A slightly old-fashioned, paternalistic attitude prevailed but it was all very jolly and everyone went home with arms full of goodies. And curiously, whatever the weather conditions had been during the run-up

Author in the
marquee at the 2005
Merrythought Open
Day, having just
officially opened the
event.

to the event, the sun always shone for Merrythought's Open Days, leading
some to joke that Oliver Holmes had friends in very high places. Sadly, much
of this bonhomie was lost when Club membership fees were scrapped.
Presumably to compensate for the subsequent loss of revenue, members were
now required to pay £10 for their Open Day ticket. It was not a vast amount,
and indeed was a good deal less than the £17.50 they had previously been
paying for annual membership, but all the same some resented having to pay

Amy Martin looks on as the facial features of a Cheeky Bear are sewn to her specifications . . .

. . . giving her a memorable souvenir of the 2006 Open Day.

Television presenter Lorne Spicer launching a special edition at the 2005 Open Day.

for a benefit that had once been free. I attended the last Open Day, held three months before the company's temporary closure, and the numbers seemed slightly down, although the jollity was still in evidence. Since the relaunch of a pared-down Merrythought, there have been two further Open Days but according to some reports they have lacked many of the elements that once made the event unmissable. Whether the glory days are gone for good, we'll just have to wait and see.

Celebrity bears and catwalk chic

There is something about Merrythought that has always attracted celebrity attention. During the 1950s, senior members of the royal family regularly visited the company's stand at toy fairs, where they would say a few gracious words and admire the new collections. This royal connection continued into the 1970s and 1980s; Prince Charles received gifts of Merrythought animals on at least two occasions and Prince Edward famously gave Prince Andrew and Sarah Ferguson an outsized Merrythought teddy bear on their wedding day. The Merrythought magic has proven even more irresistible to a biographer of some of our foremost royals, the erudite writer, broadcaster and former MP Gyles Brandreth. At his Stratford-upon-Avon Teddy Bear Museum, Brandreth had a special cabinet filled with wonderful vintage Merrythought teds. They were sold when the contents of the museum went under the

Jacqueline Revitt watches as Richard Branson poses with his namesake, Branson Bear.

hammer at Christie's in September 2007. Even a mighty business magnate like Richard Branson has seen the appeal of Merrythought bears. When Virgin Atlantic commissioned a special limited edition Cheeky called Branson Bear, he was very happy to pose for photographs with his namesake and its designer, Jacqueline Revitt. A few years later, the Isle of Man's premier teddy bear retailer, The Bear Huggery, asked Merrythought to create a Norman

Bear Huggery proprietor Carol Frazer with Norman Wisdom and the Manx Mencap bear.

Cover of the Bear Faced Chic auction catalogue.

Bear Faced Chic

Tuesday 7th
November 2000
6-30 - 9.00 pm
SOTHEBY'S

In association with

VOGUE

in aid of
Norwood
Ravenswood

Sponsored by
UBS
Private Banking

MERRYTHOUGHT

Browns

OLD
MUTUAL
OLD MUTUAL FUND MANAGERS

Wisdom Bear to raise funds for Manx Mencap. The veteran funny man is a resident of the island and he agreed to sign the bears, making them very collectable indeed. And in 2005, television presenter and collectables expert Lorne Spicer commissioned a pair of limited edition Merrythought replica bears which she promoted at that year's Open Day.

If it all sounds very show-bizzy, Merrythought's ultimate brush with glamour came in 2000 when the company was involved in an auction hosted by Sotheby's in aid of Norwood Ravenswood, a charity dedicated to helping unhappy or disadvantaged children and young people. The auction, 'Bear

Faced Chic', offered a number of special Merrythought 'catwalk' bears which Jacqueline Revitt had designed, and which were subsequently dressed in haute couture by some of the world's leading fashion houses. The company had been involved in a similar charity auction hosted by Christie's two years previously but this time the event was much more glitzy. Thanks to the endorsement of *Vogue* and the involvement of top flight committee members such as Marie Helvin, Jemima Khan, Lady Victoria Hervey, Sophie Anderton and numerous others, a host of leading designers including Emporio Armani, DKNY, Burberry, Dolce & Gabbana, Nicole Farhi, Tommy Hilfiger, Prada, Valentino and Stella McCartney agreed to dress bears for the auction. Joining the luminaries on the committee was none other than Merrythought's Oliver Holmes who must surely have enjoyed rubbing shoulders with some of the world's most gorgeous women.

CHAPTER EIGHT

Decline, Fall and Resurrection (2006–present)

Out of time

WHEN THE teddy bear celebrated its centenary in 2002, the future looked rosy for those involved in the manufacture of collectable bears. Certainly few would have predicted that within four years, Merrythought would be forced to close down temporarily before relaunching in a vastly reduced capacity. Yet the signs were there, if anyone had been looking for them. The public's appetite for limited edition bears was still strong but was lagging just a little following the deluge of commemorative bears that had appeared during the last couple of years. First the dawn of the new millennium, then the teddy bear's centenary, and following that the Queen's Golden Jubilee, all gave the industry an excuse to fall into a virtual frenzy of production, with bear after bear appearing to celebrate these occasions. Although Merrythought did not produce an unduly excessive number of commemorative bears, those that they did produce were competing with similar offerings from other popular manufacturers including Steiff, Dean's, Teddy Hermann and Hermann Spielwaren. A lot of collectors favoured one manufacturer over all the rest and remained loyal to them but there were others that bought whatever pleased them, regardless of brand. For these floating buyers, there was simply too much choice.

Nor were other manufacturers Merrythought's only competition. In the 1990s the American trend of creating highly individual teddy bears took hold in Britain and the rest of Europe, presenting collectors with an alternative to manufactured bears. Even though Merrythought was now making bears in fairly small editions, sometimes as low as 100, the artists had the upper hand

The Queen's Golden Jubilee in 2002 gave bear manufacturers something new to commemorate; Cheeky Jubilee 2002 was one such offering from Merrythought.

when it came to exclusivity as they rarely created editions larger than ten and increasingly preferred to make one-off designs. Overall, the craftsmanship of the artists was exceptionally high and although they paid high prices for the mohair, alpaca or other fur fabric from which they made their bears, working from home kept their other overheads low. This meant that their unique creations could often be purchased for not much more – and sometimes less – than a Merrythought limited edition. The advent of the internet helped the bear artists reach a potential global audience of millions. Although the same tool was available to Merrythought, it did not make the best use of it, perhaps because the company did not have an experienced marketing professional to identify and make the most of the new opportunities.

A few manufacturers responded to the bear artist threat by commissioning some of the best artists to design bears which they would then manufacture. Merrythought did not follow this route because in Jacqueline Revitt they knew they had a designer more than capable of turning out highly original designs. However, the reality was that her excellent designs were often compromised by the use of dated materials which had been over-bought years ago and needed to be used up. Another problem, in the opinion of a former member of staff, was the poor execution of the finishing touches by certain workers

Jacqueline Revitt designed many excellent and original bears like this example called Tassels, but unlike Tassels, some were not well executed when they went into production.

who had been with the company too long. Whilst remaining steadfastly loyal to Merrythought and her former colleagues, Jacqueline Revitt herself acknowledges there were problems. 'It was a shame when designs were simplified, often without my knowledge, to the degree that I sometimes did not recognise them myself,' she comments. 'A lot of collectors were always looking for that something extra in the design; after all, the card shops are full of simply styled bears and it was after all an expensive item.'

There were other indications that Merrythought was heading towards an uncertain future. The company's laudable commitment to excellence was in itself creating problems because rather than outsource the more specialist elements of toy-making, the management insisted on retaining everything in-house. While this ensured work was completed to their high standards, running a woodwork department, metal workshop, paint room and lacquer shop was very costly. A former employee believes no one will ever know the real cost of some of Merrythought's products as they were so labour intensive. 'Whilst Merrythought prided itself on telling customers their products were hand made, they simply would not have believed just how involved they were to make!' he reveals. 'The Yes/No bear mechanisms were each made, from scratch, by hand on site and all rocking horse bases were made on site.'

New members of staff were frequently astonished by the working conditions they found at Merrythought. Peter Andrews, who joined the company in 2002 as Secretary of the International Collectors' Club, admits he was stunned by the working environment. 'Merrythought was a quaint "Heartbeat" style factory where people still wore brown work coats and addressed Oliver [the Managing Director] as Mr Holmes. At first glance, Merrythought appeared a dream production facility: beautiful surroundings, long serving staff, flexible hours, paid meals and generous holidays. It was the archetypal British factory,' he concedes, 'only it was fifty years too late. In 2002 it had a Collectors' Club comprising 600 members and a respectably sized workforce. The ageing factory also boasted a separately staffed canteen, which produced toast at 11am, lunch and served tea at breaktime.'

Andrews joined just as the company was enjoying its final moments of glory, before the decline set in. Just a few months previously, staff had been working in shifts through the night in order to meet the huge demand for a little bear called 'Hope' which had been issued to raise funds for the families of 9/11 victims. Oliver Holmes had expected to sell about 400 of the 8-inch black plush bears but when Hope was featured on ITV's *This Morning* show, it made an immediate impact on viewers and sold in its thousands. It was almost certainly the last time Merrythought experienced that volume of demand.

As time progressed, the startling reality of the situation was that sales of some limited edition bears were fewer than ten. According to an insider who prefers to remain anonymous, Merrythought really needed proper crisis meetings but there were too many big personalities for such a relatively small firm. Pride, says the insider, was another factor in the company's decline – it had very little contact with its core buyers and failed to listen to retailers. 'Twenty-First Century business practices and technologies passed the company by,' they suggest, 'and key staff were not allowed the opportunity to acquire better training as paranoia set in. In truth the company desperately needed a figure with real commercial experience to come in and rock the boat. Tough decisions could have averted the ultimate end.' It seems that in order to survive in the Twenty-First Century, Merrythought first needed to embrace it. Yet, again according to the insider, there was a deluded belief that the business would be rescued by yet another chance success like Cheeky or the more recent Hope Bear. Attempts to come up with a new saviour bear proved futile, although the large orders that still came in for Cheeky from Japan, China and occasionally the USA, just about managed to keep the company afloat. As they put it, 'Never has one company had to rely on such a precarious niche product as this.'

With the first shedding of staff in 2003/2004, the writing was on the wall. Directors started to leave in the following years, and in 2005 Jacqueline Revitt's employment was abruptly terminated when she was made redundant just seventeen months away from retirement. She was, she admits, absolutely devastated. 'After all, I had been with them for thirty-four years. My whole life changed overnight and I had only three days to adjust.' When Jacqueline left, her trials machinist, a lady called Esther Walters, chose to leave with her. Esther had worked for Merrythought for fifty-four years, first as a very young machinist and then as a chargehand, but had been made redundant in one of the previous staff culls. Ironically, an increase in Jacqueline's workload meant she needed extra help so Esther returned to work with her until Jacqueline's redundancy in 2005.

While outsiders in the teddy bear industry had been watching Merrythought's performance with concern for some time, they saw the departure of Jacqueline Revitt as a sign that things were much worse than had been previously understood. When Oliver Holmes had joined Merrythought in 1972, the company could do little wrong. However, my anonymous insider stated that a series of wasted opportunities meant that when the going got really tough, there was nothing to fall back on. They cite the immense business potential Merrythought once had as UK distributor of Fisher Price toys, as well as the golden opportunity presented to the company when it was asked to design and produce the first Wallace and Gromit toys. That particular deal could have breathed new life into the factory but instead it was lost to cheaper, Oriental manufacture. 'In fact,' says the insider, 'many great opportunities were either lost or refused simply because Merrythought's

Former Club Secretary Peter Andrews with an outsized Merrythought Ballerina Bear.

senior decision-makers could not agree or were out of touch with what was happening elsewhere. Many senior staff had just spent too long there and they had little experience beyond the world of Merrythought. Naturally, personalities clashed and there was much rivalry, which ultimately let valuable business opportunities slip by.'

It's a harsh view, but then business can be a harsh environment. All the same, it is difficult not to feel sympathy for Oliver Holmes who had steered the company through the troubled waters of the 1980s and, towards the end of that decade, had recognised that the future lay in limited edition bears. That this market was now saturated to the extent that limited editions were starting to lose meaning was not his fault, and neither were the prevailing economic conditions. As stated in his December 2006 interview with Edward Heathcoat Amory of the *Daily Mail*, Merrythought started to go into decline 'within minutes of Mr Blair taking power in 1997.' His other quoted reasons for the collapse of Merrythought – red tape, high taxes, increased competition from the Far East and a toy market now dominated by a handful of big retailers – are all valid but they do not tell the whole story. Merrythought did in fact venture into Far Eastern production but could not produce too many items overseas as to do so would risk the loss of vital custom from Japan (where the Merrythought brand is regarded as a prestigious British hand-made product). Furthermore, the insider believes that many of the pieces Merrythought produced in China were poorly researched, not market tested and too expensive for a public that refuses to pay a premium for goods manufactured in China. 'The Great British Bear collection was an example of poorly researched ideas and a weak product line,' he believes. 'In all, thousands of these bears were produced in advance. A great deal of money was spent on box design, graphic design and PR, for what was a micro-sized version of an outdated 1970s bear which, despite the blatantly British name, was made in China.' The bears retailed at £24.99 and unsurprisingly sales were poor, since even the Merrythought label could not persuade people to pay over the odds for a foreign, mass-produced teddy of the sort they could buy for much less in any tourist hotspot.

When the axe finally fell, the shock felt by those that love the Merrythought name was not shared by staff past or present. Controversially, the insider believes the liquidation was both necessary and meticulously planned. His opinion is that Oliver Holmes made a harsh, yet financially sound, business decision. 'In all honesty,' he says, 'Merrythought was like watching a train crash in slow motion; you could literally see the decline day-to-day.'

Yet there is some question as to whether the closure was ever intended to be permanent. 'Whilst news of the liquidation spread,' the insider reveals, 'meetings were

Oliver Holmes in happier times, greeting visitors to a Merrythought Open Day.

being held behind the factory's boarded windows about how to start up again. Merrythought is now running as it should have done years ago; not as the toy factory it once was, but as a small-scale production facility. Let's hope it has the sense to learn from the past.'

For the employees that lost their jobs, Merrythought's closure in November 2006 was a grave misfortune and if, as has been suggested, Merrythought did fail because it remained static while the rest of the world had moved on, those employees reaped the bitter consequences. But now that the company is operating again, albeit on a smaller scale, we should be glad that the brand made famous by the likes of Clifton Rendle, Florence Attwood, Trayton Holmes, Jimmy Matthews, Jean Barber, Jacqueline Revitt and Oliver Holmes will once more fly the flag for the British soft toy industry.

CHAPTER NINE

Not Just Bears

Who let the dogs out?

ALTHOUGH teddy bears have always been a significant part of Merrythought's output, they do not represent the whole story because from the very beginning, other types of soft toy were also important. Animals, dolls, gollies, gnomes, pixies and even Humpty Dumpty have all made appearances in the Merrythought range at one time or another. Dogs featured particularly heavily in the catalogues of the early years. In fact, the first item to appear in the 1931 catalogue was Greyfriars Bobby, a Skye Terrier toy made from natural long pile plush. Bobby was inspired by Eleanor Atkinson's popular book concerning the real Greyfriars Bobby, a dog so devoted to his master that when the latter died, Bobby slept on his grave in Greyfriars churchyard in Edinburgh every night until his own death many years later. The faithful animal became so famous that he was given the freedom of the city and after his death a memorial was erected to his memory. Merrythought's version of Greyfriars Bobby was a handsome toy which could be purchased either sitting or standing, with each option available in a choice of two sizes. Sitting Bobby measured 7.5 or 8.5 inches high while the standing version was 10 or 12 inches. It seems Merrythought set much store by Greyfriars Bobby and expected him to be a big commercial success because in addition to appearing in the catalogue immediately after the title page, he turned up again in greater detail on page nine. At 150 shillings per dozen for the 12-inch standing version, he was far and away the most expensive item in that first catalogue. By contrast, the 12.5-inch Magnet Bear – referred to as 'a really cheap line' – cost 42 shillings per dozen while the more expensive Merrythought Bear cost 60 shillings per dozen for the 13-inch version. At this remove it is impossible to know if sales of Greyfriars Bobby lived up to Merrythought's expectations but the fact that he was removed from the catalogue after 1933 suggests he might not have been a total success. Today he is a rare collectors' item and would generate a lot of interest should he come up for sale at auction.

Greyfriars Bobby was just the first in a very long line of Merrythought dogs.

Brown art silk dachshund,
1970s, 14 inches long.

In the end, so many breeds were represented that if a collector chose to concentrate solely on them, it could take years to find them all, especially if examples in good condition were wanted. Some are far easier to find than others. Poodles were made in large quantities in the 1950s and 1960s and remain fairly easy to find today, as does the lovely Doleful Spaniel which first appeared in 1964. On the other hand, Scottish Terriers (Scotties) dating from the 1930s can take some tracking down. Not unnaturally, the earlier the item, usually the harder it is to find. Below is an alphabetical list of dog breeds Merrythought created from 1931 to the mid-1980s (not including character dogs from television, film etc):

Aberdeen Terrier
Basset Hound
Bloodhound
Boxer
Cairn Terrier
Chow
Collie
Dachshund
Fox Terrier
Irish Terrier
Old English Sheep Dog
Poodle
Scottish Terrier
Sealyham Terrier
St. Bernard
Wirehaired Fox Terrier

Afghan Hound
Bedlington Terrier
Border Collie
Bulldog
Chihuahua
Cocker Spaniel
Corgi
Dalmatian
Great Dane
Maltese
Pekingese
Schnauzer
Setter
Skye Terrier
West Highland Terrier

It's an impressive list, made even more so when the Merrythought versions of various character dogs from film and television are added to it. Usually the non-character dogs were referred to in the catalogues by breed name but some were given individual names which were, by and large, perfectly innocuous, such as Angus, Patch, Spot and Garry. However, a sweet-looking, brown art silk spaniel pup in the 1931 catalogue was lumbered with the name Bogey, which while it must have been entirely acceptable in its day would raise a snigger today. Nor was Bogey the worst name to feature in the catalogue; that dubious honour belongs to Pimpo, an elephant made from either grey or pink and blue art silk. It has to be said that the dodgy name didn't seem to do him any harm because Pimpo remained in the range until 1937.

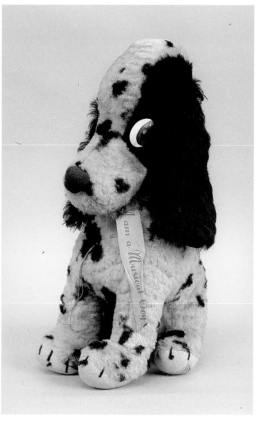

13.25-inch musical Doleful Spaniel, 1960s–1970s, made from artificial silk and mohair.

8-inch Boxer Pup and 10-inch Cheshire Cat with rubber face, both dating from the 1960s.

Artists of renown

From the very beginning, Merrythought commissioned well known artists to design toys for them, starting in 1931 with Chloe Preston. A successful children's illustrator of independent means, Preston was best known for creating chubby, big-eyed child characters called The Peek-a-Boos. Her illustrations appeared in books, on postcards, posters, prints and china, and during the 1930s she designed toys for both Merrythought and Farnell. Her first for Merrythought was Foo-Foo, a charming little dog of indeterminate breed. In 1932 Foo-Foo was joined by a kitten called Ki-Ki and a few years later by Dinkie, another dog. Dinkie, a rather mischievous-looking pup, was an established Chloe Preston character which was also manufactured by Farnell in the 1930s. Over the years Merrythought made him in four different sizes, none bigger than 7.5 inches, and offered him in various shades of velvet. He appears to have been enduringly popular as Merrythought continued to make him until 1959.

The list of illustrators who went on to work with Merrythought, either by creating original characters or allowing them to produce toy versions of existing ones, contains many names that are still revered today, including Cecil Aldin, G.E. Studdy (creator of Bonzo), Lawson Wood, Lilian Rowles,

Lawson Wood's Gran'pop was a hit for Merrythought; the eyes on this example are not original.

Mabel Lucie Atwell and her daughter, Peggy Earnshaw. One Lawson Wood character, an artful ginger ape called Gran'pop, featured in annuals which were popular all over the world, giving Merrythought a global market for their versions of him. They made their first Gran'pop in 1938 and apart from a brief hiatus during the war years, continued producing him until 1964.

Although their output of characters created by leading illustrators was prolific, Merrythought sometimes obtained licensing rights from authors rather than illustrators, as with Enid Blyton's Noddy (produced from 1958 to 1968) and Big Ears (produced 1958 to 1962). Although Harmsen van der Beek drew the original Noddy illustrations, the rights clearly remained with Blyton as she is named as the designer in the Merrythought trials book.

Good Golly, Miss Dolly

Whilst the majority of people familiar with the Merrythought name are more likely to associate it with teddy bears than dolls, aficionados know that the company has a long track record of producing dolls, gollies and other figural toys, many of which are really rather gorgeous. The first golly appeared in the catalogue in 1932 where it was referred to as a 'golliwog' and described as 'a really jolly Golly'. The blurb called it 'A modern up-to-the-minute version of an old-fashioned favourite' and went on to say it was 'Dressed throughout in best quality art silk plush'. The jolly golly was available in three size options – 16, 18.5 and 22.5 inches – and cost 10, 15 and 21 shillings each respectively,

a pricing structure that made the golly a bit of a luxury item. From 1932 onwards gollies maintained a fairly constant presence in the Merrythought range until the mid-1970s when accusations of political incorrectness forced them into the wilderness. There they remained until the age of the collector brought them out of exile. To this day they remain a contentious issue for some people while others adore them and collect absolutely anything with a golly theme. Early Merrythought gollies are not that difficult to find but they are frequently very worn, and their popularity with collectors pushes prices up for examples in better condition.

'Mr Jingles' golly, 20 inches, circa 1967–1979.

This 1960s golly is fitted with a 'tingaling' sound.

It is not possible to record every Merrythought doll design in this book but since their pre-World War Merrythought dolls were little works of art, it is worth taking a closer look at some of them. Those produced from 1936 to 1939 were detailed and imaginative while the earlier designs tended to be quite basic. The very first doll, burdened with the criminally twee name of 'Cuddly Coo', was nothing more than a doll's face on top of a comfortably round body made from art silk or woolly plush. As Cuddly Coo was marketed as 'the ideal toy for the tiny baby', much was made of the fact that it was 'Soft, light and cuddlesome, with washable face'. Reassuringly for a baby's toy, there was 'Nothing to hurt'.

Cuddly Coo was part of a range called Teenie Toys which was fairly eclectic as it also included Baby Bingie, Squirrel, Sitting Kid and Sitting Rabbit, as well as Gnome, another doll-type toy. Although his jointed legs made him a more sophisticated toy than Cuddly Coo, it is doubtful if his pointy gnome-like features made him popular with the very small babies he was intended to please. While Cuddly Coo and Gnome both made it into the 1933 catalogue, they were joined by some new doll designs which were much more baby-friendly. Tinkabell (nothing to do with Peter Pan's fairy friend) was a soft, unjointed baby doll with sideways-glancing eyes and a fitted voice that said 'Mama'; Eska Doll was dressed in a furry snow suit with pompoms on the front; Bunting Doll was similar to Eska Doll but wore a furry one-piece instead of Eska's integral tunic and trousers; and finally, Pixie was very similar to Tinkabell but was made from crushed artificial silk plush. All four new designs came in a number of different size options, indicating that Merrythought expected to see a lot of interest in them. Pixie appears to have lived up to expectations the most, becoming so popular that two different nightdress case versions were soon added to the range.

The next big development in Merrythought's doll production came in 1936 when the catalogue offered four pages of dolls. The usual complement of baby dolls was present but additionally, for the first time a number of more elaborate designs were included. Merrythought called them character dolls and introduced them in a more than usually fulsome manner. 'These are the "People" you can be sure of taking a leading part in the play room "Adventures",' they proclaimed. 'They roam the plains, sail the seas, tumble in everyone's way at the circus and charm the "Let's Pretend Pantomime." All the other ordinary Dollies will enjoy their company – so will the Kiddies.' Clearly it was hoped that these dolls – a cowboy, sailor, harlequin and clown – would inspire a great deal of imaginative play. Velvet of different colours was used for all the designs but Buddy, the cowboy doll, was also made from plush and felt. The following year a new character, Turkish Delight, was added to the range; resembling a Turkish man wearing traditional costume including a fez, it was made from brightly coloured art silk plush. Also in 1937, a range of 8-inch character dolls called 'Little People' was introduced, amongst which was King Cole, Puck, Topsy (a black doll wearing a grass skirt) and 'Yah Sah', a black chef. In 1938 there were two Merrythought catalogues. In the first of these, little had changed in the doll lines but in the second, two

fabulous Snow White designs by Lilian Rowles were unveiled, presumably to
tie in with the full length animation feature film which Disney released that
year. A new batch of Little People also appeared alongside the earlier designs
and at 9 inches high, they were a little bigger than the originals. There were
six of these new designs, all of them designed by G.E. Studdy (see Artists of
Renown, above) and they included Simple Simon, Farmer's Boy, Eskimo and

MERRYTHOUGHT VERYLYTE   Toys

" Baby Royal "

1825 / 2, size 14"=35.5 c/m long

Body is pink stockinette, suit (which takes
off) wool crochette, colours : cream, pink
and blue. Very soft and cuddly.

Goes to sleep.

The sleeping eye, soft cuddly doll, is an
exclusive Merrythought production.

Filled soft pure kapok and fitted w
baby cry squeaker.

" Dimples "

A Baby's soft Doll. Coloured plushes, fitted
with squeaker.

1767 / 1, size 9"=23 c/m long
      / 2, „ 11"=28 „   „

" Bunting " Doll

Coloured plushes.

1201 / 2, size 15"=38 c/m high

Baby-type dolls as
featured in
Merrythought's
1950 catalogue.

Sizes are approximate

Pixie Man. There is no denying Studdy's Little People were powerful designs but the facial features – bright staring eyes and wide, grinning mouths – were more than a little scary. Far more appealing, for children at least, were 1939's Fairy Tale Art Dolls which measured 14 inches high and were made from felt. Despite the name, not all represented characters from fairy tales, with Alice in Wonderland originating from the book of the same name and at least three of the others featuring in nursery rhymes. One character that truly did come from a fairy tale, Little Red Riding Hood, had first been interpreted as a Merrythought doll back in 1934 but was reworked for the Fairy Tale Art Dolls collection. The move into production of this type of character might have come about as a result of special orders received by theatre companies. It is known that 'Jack' and 'Jill' dolls were made by Merrythought in the 1930s exclusively for pantomime impresario Emile Littler. The dolls were sold to children at theatres where the 'Jack and Jill' panto was being performed and it is possible that their popularity encouraged Merrythought to bring that kind of doll into the general range.

Furry, ferocious and feathered friends

Dogs may have been one of the mainstays of the Merrythought range but other animals have also featured heavily over the years. On the domestic front, cats and rabbits were especially popular. In the 1931 catalogue the rabbits far outnumbered the cats but the feline numbers gradually increased although they never quite overtook the bunnies. Some delightful dressed rabbits which were produced in the 1950s are not hard to find today, although very often they are missing their orig-inal garments. Various farm animals also appeared in large numbers, as did British wild animals like foxes, badgers, frogs, seals and so on. More exotic species featured too, including

17-inch 'Reynard' fox, circa 1950s/1960s, together with 8-inch Scamp (from Disney's *Lady and the Tramp*).

elephants, tigers, leopards, zebras, monkeys, giraffes, crocodiles, rhinos and, one of Merrythought's most memorable animal toys, a soft green hippo made from nylon plush. First introduced in 1967, the comical hippo captured the public's affection to such an extent that it became a fixture in the range until 1985. It was made in a number of different sizes, the smallest of which – and most commonly found – measures 9 inches while the largest is 40 inches. Many people have fond memories of these green hippos but because they were made in such large numbers they are widely available today on the secondary market and are therefore very inexpensive.

Dressed 'Mr Bumpkin' badger and mole, from a series made in 1985.

Included in Merrythought's vast menagerie of animals are a number of feathered friends. Most fall into a category which could loosely be described as poultry or fowl – hens, chicks, cockerels, ducks, mallards, geese etc – and then there are a few exotics such as penguins, pelicans, toucans, parakeets, parrots and puffins. Also represented are some of the UK's native wild birds including a magpie, two owls, a woodpecker and a kingfisher. Even a few humble insects have received the Merrythought treatment, although only the child-friendly, easy-on-the-eye sort like ladybirds, bumble-bees and caterpillars.

'Woosie' cat, 17 inches, circa 1934.

All the toys mentioned above were intended for cuddling or display but Merrythought also produced an enormous range of animal toys which could be ridden, rocked, pulled or pushed along. Thanks to the on-site metal and woodwork departments, these toys were made entirely on the premises to

Merrythought's green hippos were playroom favourites throughout the 1970s and early 1980s.

Trying out a rocking-horse at the 2006 Open Day.

extremely high standards. The first were made in the 1930s and some production continued right up until the last few years, so several generations of children grew up with a Merrythought rocking-horse or push-along toy in their nursery. Sadly these super toys are no longer being made but they can sometimes be found at salerooms, on internet auction sites or even at antique centres.

Stars of film and television

Quite apart from their excursions into Disney territory (which are listed below), Merrythought have had a long history of creating much-loved characters from both the big and small screen. They began in 1951 with the creation of a 6.5-inch velveteen 'Jerry' from MGM's Tom and Jerry cartoons. Oddly enough, fans of the cartoon had to wait three years until a Tom came along for Jerry to torment. The next character offerings, penguins Bobo and Father from a little-remembered black and white television show called *Meet the Penguins*, appeared in 1954. Rin Tin Tin followed in 1958 but things did not really get going until the 1960s when the floodgates opened with the arrival of characters such as Deputy Dawg, Mr Jinks and Muskie (all from *Deputy Dawg and Friends*) and Huckleberry Hound, Yogi Bear, Pixie and Dixie (from *Huckleberry Hound and Friends*). These characters were all from American shows, the sole British offering of the decade being Harry Corbett's Sooty, although Italy also got in on the act with Maria Perego's enchanting mouse, Topo Gigio. In the 1970s, however, more offerings from home-grown television started to appear

This Pixie and Dixie nightdress case dates from the 1960s.

with Merrythought producing versions of Dougal from *The Magic Roundabout*, Parsley the Lion from *The Herbs* and Mungo and Midge from *Mary, Mungo and Midge*. A rather cool, 17-inch Pink Panther also made a brief appearance early in the 1970s.

Walt Disney

Surely one of Merrythought's greatest coups over the years must have been securing the rights to create characters from Disney films and cartoons. Although these rights did not extend world-wide, they covered a wide swathe of global territory including the Middle and Far East and Australia, as well as Great Britain itself. From 1954 until 1980, Merrythought produced a parade of important Disney characters and thanks, perhaps, to the Disney organisation's stringent quality requirements, they represent some of the company's best work. This is another area in which

Merrythought/Walt Disney Designs 'Pluto', 14 inches, from 1972.

collectors can choose to specialise, although as with dogs they are likely to find certain pieces harder to find than others. Dating from the 1960s, Winnie the Pooh and his Hundred Acre Wood pals crop up at fairs and auctions fairly regularly, as do Lady and Tramp. To acquire the delightful Snow White and the Seven Dwarfs, however (produced from 1954 to 1955), patience, determination and a healthy bank balance are essential. The full list of Disney/Merrythought characters is given below, together with the films or cartoons from which the characters originated.

101 Dalmatians:	Lucky; unnamed Floppy Dalmatian
Bambi:	Bambi and Thumper
Dumbo The Flying Elephant:	Dumbo
Lady and the Tramp:	Lady, Tramp and Scamp
Old Yeller:	Old Yeller
Snow White:	Snow White; Doc; Dopey; Happy; Sleepy; Sneezy; Grumpy; Bashful

Various cartoons:	Donald Duck; Mickey Mouse; Minnie Mouse; Pluto
Winnie the Pooh (various feature films):	Winnie the Pooh; Eeyore; Kanga and Roo; Rabbit; Piglet; Wol; Tigger

Chapter Ten

Is it a Merrythought?

IF YOU'RE thinking of buying a Merrythought teddy bear, it is essential to do some research beforehand or you may end up spending a considerable sum of money on something that is not what you think it is. The first thing to do is decide whether you want a bear produced before or after the Second World War, then learn to recognise the characteristics typical of bears from your chosen era. Generally speaking, the following guidelines apply to traditional teddy designs (but remember that exceptions do occur, especially with the labels, and different characteristics apply to specific designs such as Bingie, Cheeky etc).

Trio of 1930s bears showing different materials used for paw pads – velveteen, felt and oilcloth.

Pre-Second World War

- Muzzles are pronounced and shaven
- Arms are long and gently curving
- Legs have chubby thighs
- Ears are usually large, flat and sewn across the top of the bear's head on most of the standard designs
- Glass eyes, frequently amber and black
- Noses are stitched vertically, often with the two outermost stitches on either side dropping below the others; there is, however, one teddy design which has a horizontally stitched nose
- Many bears made from good quality golden mohair
- Gold and brightly coloured artificial silk plush also used for bears
- Pads are wool felt, velveteen or sometimes oilcloth
- Paws have four short-ish stitched claws which are webbed

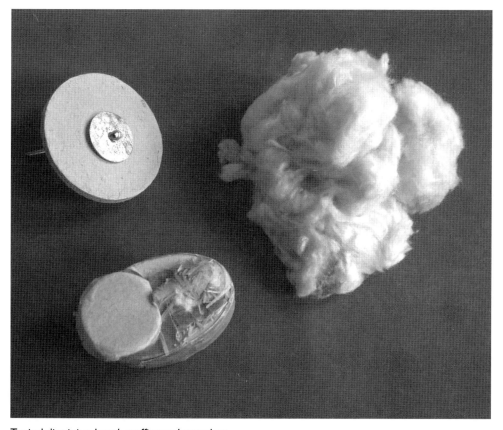

Typical disc joint, kapok stuffing and squeaker.

- Mouths are stitched in an inverted Y shape
- Stuffing is kapok/woodwool mix
- Celluloid-covered metal buttons used, fixed sometimes to ears and sometimes to backs
- Embroidered, woven labels stitched to left or right feet; wording reads 'Merrythought hygienic toys made in England' or simply 'made in England by Merrythought' on earliest bears

Post-Second World War*

- Muzzles are flatter and unshaven
- Arms are shorter and straighter
- Legs are shorter and the chubby thighs have gone
- Plastic safety eyes are used

*Apart from bears produced in the years just after the end of the war/early 1950s which tend to resemble those made before 1939

Close-up of typical amber and black glass eyes.

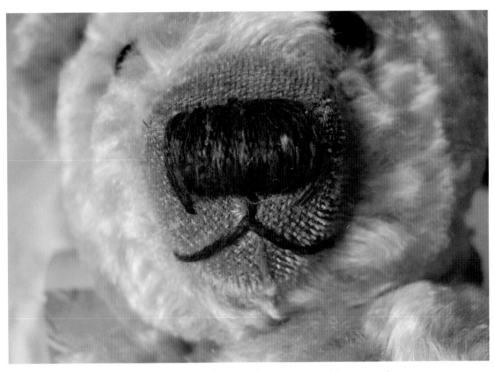

Dropped vertical outermost stitches are a feature of many pre-war Merrythought noses.

Celluloid-covered metal buttons were fixed to ears or to backs.

Early Merrythought label.

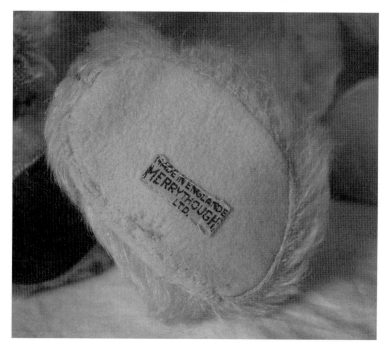

Alternative early
Merrythought label.

- Webbed claw stitching fades out, and claws gradually disappear altogether
- London Gold mohair used from 1965
- Button no longer in use

Typical post-war traditional bear in London Gold mohair.

Post-war label widely used up to 1991.

Wishbone label used from 1992.

- Printed yellow labels with wording 'Merrythought Ironbridge, Shrops. Made in England' used until 1991
- Alternative white label with same wording as above and additional 'Regd Design' used up to the 1990s
- Embroidered label with wording 'Merrythought Ironbridge, Shropshire, Made in England' plus wishbone symbol used from 1992
- Some modern labels read 'Hand made in England'

At a glance

It may sound obvious but the best way to positively identify a Merrythought bear is by a label, so

Alternative post-war label.

if you are adamant that nothing but a Merrythought will do for you it may be best to pass on any unlabelled bears you find. This is because the absence of a label or button can make it very difficult to say with certainty that a particular bear was made by Merrythought, since several manufacturers made very similar designs. Familiarity with the overall shape of Merrythought bears can help, but they share many characteristics with bears from other companies – like Chad Valley's teddies, for example, their ears were positioned across the top of their heads – so this won't in itself prove anything. The growlers and squeakers used by Merrythought were also used by most of the other teddy manufacturers; even Chad Valley's patented 'Grunter' was sold to their rivals so the presence of one inside a bear does not necessarily mean it was not made by Merrythought. The glass eyes used by Merrythought were also standard so they are no help in the identification process and, in the case of musical bears, neither are the Swiss-made music boxes which were used by most of the leading manufacturers.

With older bears, the strongest clue that you are looking at a Merrythought teddy bear will be the presence of webbed claw stitching. This type of claw stitching was also used by Farnell but their bears had five stitched claws as opposed to Merrythought's four, and Farnell's claws were more pointed and sweeping (see claw comparisons in Chapter 2). So, if you find a bear with four webbed claws, there's a good chance it will have been made by Merrythought, but before you rush to buy it, just make sure the other features tally with what you would expect to find on a Merrythought bear of this period. As for later bears, vast amounts were made from London Gold mohair which has a short, dense pile and is bright, almost brassy, in colour. If you learn to recognise London Gold you stand a good chance of spotting a later Merrythought bear.

Sometimes bears that appear unlabelled contain a hidden secret. If their pads have been replaced because the original material was badly worn, it is worth carefully unpicking the replacement pads in case remnants of the originals remain, together with an all-important label. To know if the pads are original, study them carefully. Original felt pads should have worn thinner with age and they will have irregular discolouration in places; brown felt pads often go mottled with age. A bear's foot pads are likely to be paler than the paw pads because over many years of the bear sitting on a chair or a shelf the feet tend to be more exposed to the light. Thick, bright felt pads which are of a uniform colour are likely to be modern replacements.

Is the bear 'right'?

Ever since old teddy bears hit the spotlight and began to command high prices, a few unscrupulous individuals have sought ways to cheat the unwary. That is why it is so important to do your homework before you start collecting, and even then it is as well to make sure you only buy from reputable dealers. Not only do good dealers have immense knowledge about vintage bears, which they are usually very happy to share with novice collectors, they also value their reputations far too much to knowingly cheat a customer. The majority provide detailed receipts, invaluable for insurance purposes, and give automatic refunds in the unlikely event that the bear is not as advertised. If you don't know any old bear dealers, visit the big bear fairs and talk to the people you see buying old bears. Arctophiles are a friendly bunch and will be glad to share their experiences with you. You can also refer to the Directory at the back of this book for some suggestions.

Of course there are plenty of other sources for old bears and since some of them are not as reliable as the expert dealers, it is useful to know about a few of the potential scams. One of the easiest to spot involves labels: an earlier Merrythought label, probably removed from a very worn out toy animal, is sewn onto a later teddy bear. The bear is then offered for sale at a price reflecting its 'early' date. By understanding and recognising the design features of early Merrythought teddies (see guidelines, above) potential buyers can avoid falling into this trap. Even when labels do exist, uninformed vendors sometimes describe bears as older than they actually are in the belief that an older bear will be more expensive. I vividly recall a non-specialist antiques dealer assuring me that the Cheeky Bear I was examining dated from the 1930s, apparently blissfully unaware that Cheeky did not appear until 1957.

A more sophisticated scam occurs when a Merrythought bear which is sold as 'all original' has lost most or all of the original kapok stuffing, and so modern stuffing has been used instead. To tell if a bear has had its kapok stuffing replaced or topped up, get hold of it and feel it all over. Modern poly-ester-based stuffing will feel much bouncier to the touch than kapok which is soft but settles and has more resistance. Of course, you may be prepared to accept a bit of replacement stuffing but even so the vendor should tell you about it so you can make an informed decision. (You can't do this if you're buying over the internet so make sure the vendor offers a no quibbles money-back guarantee.)

A worse scenario than a bit of replaced stuffing is a 'marriage', a scam in which parts of different bears have been sewn together to make a whole bear. After you've handled a lot of Merrythought bears you should get a sixth sense that tells you when something is wrong but you can also check by looking for seams in unusual places. If you are in any doubt, quiz the vendor and if you don't like the answer, walk away from the purchase.

Perhaps the nastiest old bear scam involves tricking collectors into parting with large amounts of money for bears that come with detailed provenance. In recent years a bear's provenance – that is, documentary information relating to a previous owner, often including a photo – has become very important to some collectors, so much so that fairly ordinary bears with excel-lent provenance can sell for far more than their normal market value. Lots of bears are sold with perfectly genuine provenance but unfortunately a few greedy individuals have spotted the potential to make some money by faking it. Few dealers or auction houses will knowingly sell bears with dodgy prove-nance but the fakers can be clever, so the bear buyer needs to be even cleverer. Examine all claims of provenance carefully, particularly any photos claiming to show the original owner with the bear. Even allowing for the passage of time, the bear in the photo should be recognisable as the one being sold; if it isn't, be very suspicious. Also, look at any documents that pertain to the bear – these could be letters, postcards, diary entries etc – and make sure the dates tally with the bear's age. Finally, if the bear is being sold on behalf of someone else, ask if you can speak to them to verify the story. If you remain uncon-vinced, you'll need to decide if you like the bear enough to buy it for the stated price even if the provenance cannot be substantiated. Remember that, as with any commodity, a vintage teddy is only worth what someone is willing to pay for it.

Caring for your Merrythought bear

It's an unfortunate truth that teddy bears made of mohair and other natural fur fibres can make an irresistible meal for moth larvae and carpet beetles, while animal fleas are happy to make themselves at home in their fur. In order to protect bears from these shudder-inducing infestations, it is important to take certain precautions.

First steps

When you bring a vintage teddy bear into your home, the first thing you should do is ensure it is bug-free. This is especially important if you have other

Proceed with caution when cleaning coloured bears.

teddies in your house as an infestation could spread to them. The simplest thing to do is pop the newcomer in the freezer for about 48 hours; it sounds brutal but this method is highly effective and if it could speak, the teddy would probably thank you for doing it. This is my tried and trusted way of debugging a bear:

- Pop bear into clean polythene bag, either clear or plain white
- Seal the bag
- Place sealed bag inside another clean polythene bag
- Put bag-wrapped bear into deep freeze and leave it for 48 hours
- Remove wrapped bear from freezer and allow to defrost gently and naturally
- When completely defrosted, take bear to sink and brush softly to dislodge any debris from the fur

Cleaning dirty teds

Vintage bears bought on the secondary market can often look grubby but this should not deter you from buying them since mohair cleans up really well. The crucial thing to remember when washing an old teddy bear is not to immerse it in water or get it too wet. This is my method for cleaning old teddies:

- Fill a bowl with warm water and add some wool wash detergent
- Agitate with hand to create lots of lathery suds
- Place bear on clean white towel (not coloured as this could stain it)
- Put some suds on a clean white cotton cloth and dab this over bear's fur; dirt will come off onto the cloth as you work
- Be very careful not to soak bear with water, just use suds
- When bear is clean enough, towel dry it gently
- Allow to finish drying naturally or pop in airing cupboard if in a hurry
- Once dry, fluff up bear's mohair, then you're done

Note: take extra care if cleaning a bear with coloured mohair in case it isn't colour fast. Make sure the water isn't too hot, and test on a hidden patch of mohair before proceeding further.

Protection against infestation

Once you've debugged and cleaned your bear, you need to protect it from further moth attacks. Mothballs can be effective in protecting teddies from unwanted guests but they do have a strong, not altogether pleasant smell.

Old bears like this that are very worn can be protected from further damage by keeping them behind glass or covering their fur with clothes.

Luckily, there are some natural, sweeter smelling solutions you can use. Moths hate the aroma of both cedar wood and lavender, and both are used in various products including moth repellent balls, hangers, drawer sachets and sticks, all of which are widely available. Or you could make your own lavender bags which will look pretty and smell sweet as they help protect your bears from moths. Moth traps are also available.

General advice

- To prevent fur fading, keep bears out of sunlight
- Brush teddies regularly to remove dust, and check for nasty surprises
- Really valuable bears are best kept behind glass
- Don't allow anyone to smoke anywhere near your teddies as cigarette smoke can leave them smelling like an ashtray
- Teds with worn mohair can be protected from further damage by covering the worn patches with clothing
- Keep dogs well away from precious teds – they can wreak havoc in an instant
- To lessen the risk of moth attack, doors and windows to rooms in which bears are stored should be closed when outside doors/windows are open, and lights in these rooms should be switched off as moths are attracted to bright light

CHAPTER ELEVEN

Memorable Merrythoughts

Special relationships

THE SUCCESS of a manufacturer ultimately depends on its ability to find quality sales outlets, and then to foster and maintain good relations with those outlets. Over the years many retailers, large and small, have stocked Merrythought's products and all have had a part to play in the company's history, but some have been more influential than others. Of those, two very different retailers, Harrods and Teddy Bears of Witney, have arguably done more to aid Merrythought's fortunes than any others.

Merrythought's association with Harrods dates back to September 1932 when a 13-inch teddy was designed specially for the world famous Knightsbridge department store. In fact, Harrods had been extremely influential in popularising the teddy bear when it first arrived in Britain in the early 1900s. The store took delivery of its first consignment of German teddies in 1905 and immediately recognised its potential, so much so that they agreed to include them in their next catalogue. In 1910, the first British-made teddy bears (made by J.K. Farnell) appeared in the Harrods range, and in 1914, when hostilities with Germany brought a ban on German imports, the store looked to other British manufacturers for their soft toys. Thus when Merrythought set up in 1930, Harrods had a track record of selling quality, British-made teddy bears and they probably looked favourably on the new venture because of their existing relationship with former Farnell employee, Henry Janisch.

For many years thereafter Harrods stocked Merrythought's child-oriented teddies and soft toys, and when collectors' bears appeared on the scene, the store responded by commissioning exclusives and limited editions from Merrythought. Pat Rush, journalist, teddy bear enthusiast and author of *More Merrythought Magic*, remembers the excitement in 1990 when Merrythought produced a beautiful, boxed limited edition bear to celebrate their Diamond

Jubilee. 'It meant that at last British enthusiasts had access to something special,' Pat recalls:

> *I couldn't wait. The launch was to take place at Harrods in London, and I was there when the doors opened, determined to acquire the lowest possible number in the edition. Unfortunately, Harrods didn't appear to have realised that people would be so concerned about such a detail. And, as I was actually there in a somewhat official capacity – as editor of the new* Hugglets Teddy Bear Magazine *– I did not feel that I could set to and demolish the huge display of handmade boxes that the shop had set up for the occasion.*
>
> *I'd taken my friend from Northampton with me, and we both circled uncertainly until another collector actually voiced her disappointment. She had got there early because she specifically wanted the number that corresponded to the year of her birth (49, if I remember rightly). The Harrods sales person was distraught – until my friend and I offered to help find the number in question. I seem to remember that it took us less than a minute – and of course, purely by 'chance', I also managed to unearth number 5 along the way. Fortunately, no one seemed at all perturbed by the jumble of boxes we left in our wake.*
>
> *After that, I could often be found in Harrods in my lunch breaks from my full-time publishing job nearby. The firm stocked a number of special editions made by* Merrythought *and within a year there were also all the designs from the new International Collectors' Catalogue to choose from.*

With sales of teddy bears in 1997 responsible for one-third of all toys sold by Merrythought, the potential for Merrythought was immense. For a lot of collectors, the combination of Harrods and Merrythought was irresistible and they eagerly snapped up every collaborative bear that came on the market. Tourists in particular liked to be able to buy an English-made bear from a famous English store (albeit one owned by an Egyptian). The Harrods account must have been immeasurably important to Merrythought, and yet somewhere along the way things went wrong: today the store does not sell Merrythought products. According to a spokesperson in the Toy Department, this is because since their 2006 closure and subsequent reopening, Merrythought is no longer big enough to supply large accounts. This may be true, but the company still manages to supply Teddy Bears of Witney with smallish limited editions (see below) so presumably they could do the same for Harrods.

Another possible reason for the absence of Merrythought bears on the shelves at Harrods is that perhaps latterly they were not selling particularly well. As far as the collectors' market goes, it seems likely that they were losing ground to Steiff. The German firm has always had a good relationship with Harrods but in recent years, thanks to particularly effective marketing, that

2005 Merrythought/Harrods teddy bear; bears such as this were once very popular with collectors.

relationship seems to have become even stronger. Certainly, when confirming that they no longer sell Merrythought bears, the Toy Department spokesperson was keen to point me in the direction of a new Steiff limited edition.

While Merrythought's special relationship with Harrods is now a thing of the past, its association with Teddy Bears of Witney, the UK's most famous specialist teddy bear retailer, is still going strong thanks to Ian Pout, the shop's proprietor, who is a staunch advocate of the Ironbridge company: 'We are delighted that one British teddy bear manufacturer still flourishes nearly eighty years after it was founded, and especially in face of formidable Far East manufacturing competition in recent years,' he told me. 'When we opened in 1985 as England's first shop to specialise in selling new and old teddy bears, it was imperative that we should stock Merrythought bears. There were simply no other British-made traditional bears to compare in quality with theirs. Not only that, but the design of the company's bears, virtually unchanged for fifty years, made any of their "London Gold" range the archetypal English teddy bear.'

Nearly twenty-five years after the shop opened, Ian Pout is still supporting Merrythought by commissioning them to make lots of exclusive limited bears. For example, five years ago when it was decided to create a replica of Timmy, the 1940s Chiltern teddy which had been Ian's own childhood bear, it was to Merrythought he turned and more recently,

Merrythought created this replica of a Farnell featured in Pauline Cockrill's *Teddy Bear Encyclopedia* as an exclusive for Teddy Bears of Witney.

Merrythought's replica of Aloysius (foreground) enjoying a day out with the original.

Quirky designs such as Patchwork Punkie can be found at Teddy Bears of Witney as well as the more traditional offerings.

when actual size replicas were required of Aloysius, the teddy bear star of Granada Television's glorious 1981 *Brideshead Revisited* adaptation, once again Merrythought was chosen for the job.

And, in addition to traditional Merrythought bears like Aloysius and Timmy, Teddy Bears of Witney is filled with many of their iconic Cheeky and Punkinhead Bears which, says Ian, are both different and fun. 'We rejoice that they are still made in England!' he states emphatically.

Auction highlights

When people started collecting vintage teddy bears in a serious way in the 1980s, the major auction houses were quick to cotton on to the trend. Most already included the occasional old teddy in their sales but the growing interest in bear-collecting encouraged them to think for the first time about specialist sales dedicated solely to bears and soft toys. The first of these specialist sales took place at Christie's South Kensington in December 1993 and thereafter, although other auction houses also held regular teddy bear auctions, Christie's retained a special place in arctophiles' affections. Sadly, these sales were discontinued in September 2007 when policy at Christie's shifted away from the collectors' market. While they lasted, however, they were known globally as one of the best sources for interesting vintage bears, and prospective buyers routinely flew in from all over the world in order to bid for rarities.

At most teddy bear auctions held at Christie's, Steiff items almost always attracted the highest prices but amongst the British-made bears, the honours were usually shared between Merrythought and Farnell. The most in-demand Merrythoughts were always rare Cheeky variations including Mr and Mrs Twisty Cheeky, and the Punkinheads. This demand was driven by Japanese and American collectors as well as those based in the UK. In the early years of the new millennium, interest in these bears was at a peak with the result that saleroom prices went into the stratosphere. In May 2000, for example, a 10-inch, brown mohair Punkinhead wearing its original red felt shorts sold for £1,998 against a pre-sale estimate of £400 to £600. Extraordinary as this seemed, it was just a foretaste of things to come because in December 2000, a 19-inch, brown mohair Punkinhead wearing its original yellow felt shorts sold for £2,820, the sort of price more normally associated with very early Steiff bears. Again, the price far exceeded the pre-sale estimate of £600 to £800. Since then, prices have gradually fallen, perhaps because the collectors keenest to acquire Punkinheads have now obtained what they wanted. Later sales at Christie's saw prices for Punkinheads falling dramatically, with a 10-inch, brown mohair version wearing original green felt shorts selling for just £717 in December 2004. However, there is a slight possibility that prices may be on the rise again because in August 2008, a 20-inch, brown mohair Punkinhead wearing its original yellow shorts made £900 when it went under the hammer at Vectis Auctions. The higher price was probably due to the excellent

20-inch, brown
mohair Punkinhead
which sold at Vectis
in August 2008.

Christie's auctions used to be excellent places to buy Merrythought bears.

condition the bear was in and the fact that it came with provenance (informa-tion about its original owner) which is the holy grail for bear collectors.

In December 2001, a very modern Merrythought bear measuring just 7.75 inches caused something of a stir when it sold for £500 at Christie's. The amount was chicken feed in auction house terms but for a small, black, brand new bear that wasn't even made from mohair, it was an exceptional result. The bear in question was called Hope and it had been produced by Merrythought following the attack on the World Trade Center in New York on September 11th that year. Proceeds from the sale of Hope were donated to the World Trade Center Disaster Fund, and demand for the bear rocketed when it was featured on ITV's *This Morning* show and ultimately just over 16,500 were sold. The example auctioned at Christie's in December 2001 was the first in the edition. A year later, Merrythought attempted to repeat the

The little black bear that raised money for families of 9/11 victims.

success of Hope with Peace, a follow-up bear which was styled similarly to Hope but was made from white plush instead of black, and featured an embroidered white dove on its front. For every Peace Bear sold, £5 was donated to the Uniformed Firefighters Association Scholarship Fund.

Restoring a sweetheart's gift

Although it is only relatively recently that adults have been open about their passion for teddy bears, for years people have been quietly treasuring bears that hold special significance for them. Some are so dear to their owners that if any damage befalls them, the distraught owner will move heaven and earth to put things right. Frank, an early Merrythought, was one such bear. He was of no particular value but had been given to his owner by her sweetheart, also named Frank, and had been special to her ever since.

Frank (the bear, not the sweetheart) had suffered the usual wear and tear over the years but much worse was to come when his, by now elderly, owner moved house. Until her new home was ready, she needed to store some of her possessions, Frank included, at her daughter's house. However, the storage proved disastrous for poor old Frank when some hungry mice discovered him and made inroads into his face and tummy, leaving him in a desperate state. When his owner reclaimed her precious old friend and discovered the damage, she decided, after her initial shock had worn off, that the only thing to do

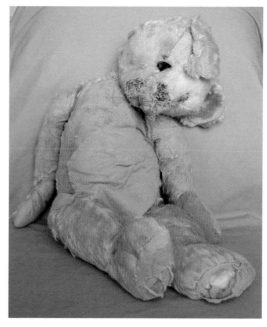

Poor old Frank before his restoration work began.

was have him professionally restored. Luckily for her, she knew of bear restorer par excellence Dot Bird (Dot's sympathetic restoration work is well known throughout the teddy bear collectors' community). Even for Dot, though, this was going to be a real challenge.

'He needed a lot of care and TLC to bring him back from the state he was in,' Dot recalls. She thought it best to begin on his head since it was very loose anyway as both joint discs had crumbled away. Frank had three holes in his muzzle that needed patching and the weaker areas needed lining. Dot found and shaved a suitable mohair fabric, cut it into three pieces then carefully sewed them into place, filling the muzzle with woodwool stuffing as she went along. 'The edges of the seams of his face were still there, allowing me to use them as a guide for the facial shape.'

Frank had pieces of black felt glued on for eyes so Dot removed these and replaced them with a new pair of suitable amber glass ones. She then restitched both his ears into position and moved on to his nose which had tiny strands of the original stitching still visible. The stitches had faded to a mid-brown shade so she dyed some cotton to match this colour and replaced his mouth and nose stitching. 'Black would have looked far too harsh on this old-timer!' she observes.

Once Frank's head was repaired Dot replaced the crumbled and broken joint discs in his arms and legs with new discs. The originals could not be

Having received expert attention, Frank's dignity was restored.

saved and would only continue to deteriorate as time went by. His legs and arms had been stuffed with a variety of different fabrics including vests, t-shirts, stockings and so on. His owner wanted them removed and replaced with the correct kapok stuffing so this was duly done. Further repairs followed – his right leg needed a patch and his paw and foot pads needed recovering with a rich tan felt that matched traces of the original felt discovered by Dot in Frank's seams. His distinctive Merrythought claw stitching was re-sewn with thread matching his nose and mouth, and then it was on to his tummy damage. There was quite a large hole under the felt cover on his tummy so poor Frank needed quite a large patch. Dot shaved yet more mohair to match his own fabric and dyed it a little to tone down the colour. This was then carefully sewn into place and a seam was sewn down the middle to match the front seams. A split in the fabric in his neck area was also repaired, and then his remaining fur was given a clean and brush. After all this, he looked more like his old, pre-mouse-snack self and was ready to return to his owner, who was delighted to have him back and promised never to put him into storage again.

Glossary

This glossary provides definitions of unusual words found in this book; it is not a complete glossary of teddy bear terminology because only terms relevant to Merrythought are included.

Alpaca:	Very soft plush made from the woven yarn of alpacas (small, South American animals that look a little like llamas)
Arctophile:	Literally a bear lover but term is frequently used to describe a teddy bear collector
Artificial silk plush:	Often referred to as 'art silk', this man-made fibre has been used for soft toy making since 1929
Celluloid:	An early plastic widely used since the 1870s; some early Merrythought bears have celluloid-covered buttons
Cotter pin:	Two-pronged metal pin used to secure disc joints
Disc joints:	Small circles of hardboard or cardboard used with cotter pins to joint teddies
Dreylon:	Better known as Dralon, this is a washable acrylic fibre which is woven into plush
Dual plush:	Mohair of one colour with the tips dyed a second colour
Glass eyes:	Blown glass eyes on wire shanks or loops widely used by soft toy industry during first half of Twentieth Century, often in amber colour with black pupils; clear eyes with black pupils were enamelled on back for colour
Hug:	Arctophiles' term for a teddy bear collection

Kapok:	A plant fibre used in many Merrythought bears; it is an excellent stuffing material because it is soft, resilient, lightweight and mould resistant
Leathercloth:	Imitation leather often used for teddy bears' paw-pads; sometimes referred to by trade name Rexine
Mohair:	A soft, silky fabric or yarn made from Angora goat hair
Nylon:	A synthetic fabric made from petroleum products, it was developed in the 1930s as an alternative to silk
Plastic:	Generic name for wide range of synthetic or semi-synthetic products; in teddy bear terminology, most often refers to eyes and noses
Plush:	Woven fabric with a thick, deep cut pile
Rexine:	See Leathercloth
Safety eyes:	Plastic eyes which lock in place by means of integral screw/shank and washer
Squeaker:	Voice-box, made from card, oilcloth, reed and a spring, which makes a squeak when squeezed
Velveteen:	Cheap velvet substitute made from woven cotton
Woodwool:	Traditional material for stuffing teddy bears, Merrythought sometimes mixed these fine shavings of soft wood with kapok to stuff their bears; it was also used to add firmness to areas such as muzzle, head etc
Wool felt:	A non-woven, natural fabric made by pressing and manipulating wool fibres

Essential
Merrythought Directory

───◈───

IF THIS book has fired your enthusiasm for Merrythought teddy bears, you may be keen to start collecting. That's great but it's best not to buy anything until you've done some homework.

For knowledge and experience of old bears, nothing beats looking at and, wherever possible, holding and examining them. Museums can be excellent places to view old teddies but their disadvantage is that since the exhibits are behind glass, you can't get hold of them and give them a thoroughly good examination. Luckily, auction viewings offer unlimited opportunities for close, hands-on inspection, and as long as you ask politely and are careful, dealers specialising in vintage bears will usually be happy to let you handle their stock. Many of these dealers exhibit at teddy bear fairs held up and down the country. It's worth getting to know the dealers, firstly because they have masses of useful information about different types of bear, and secondly because if you give them your contact details, they'll keep you informed of any interesting Merrythoughts they get in. Most dealers also operate excellent websites so once you know and trust them, you can spend many happy hours browsing online. While buying old bears online from an unknown source is not the best idea, if the website belongs to someone you know to be reputable, online shopping gives you the chance to hunt for desirable old bears whenever you want and from the comfort of your home.

The following listings include details of old bear dealers, teddy bear fairs, expert restoration, shops selling modern Merrythought bears, museums, auctioneers and useful publications. The list is by no means definitive as there are literally dozens of other reputable names that could have been included but this should help get you started. Happy hunting!

Auctioneers

- Bonhams – hold regular toy sales that include vintage teddy bears, both at their Knightsbridge, London saleroom and at Knowle in the Midlands. www.bonhams.com/toys
- Vectis – regular sales of all types of teddy bears and soft toys including vintage, modern limited editions and artist-made bears. www.vectis.co.uk

Fairs

- Winter BearFest (February) and Teddies Festival (September) – organised by Hugglets Festivals, these events which are held at Kensington Town Hall in London are widely regarded as the UK's best teddy bear fairs. www.hugglets.co.uk
- The London International Antique and Artist Dolls, Toys, Miniatures & Teddy Bear Fairs – organised by Granny's Goodies Fairs and held four times a year at Kensington Town Hall in London – www.grannys-goodiesfairs.com
- The Great Doll & Teddy Fair – organised by Debbie Woodhouse and held three times a year at the National Motorcycle Museum, Bickenhill, Nr. Birmingham. Telephone 01530 274377 or 07973 760881
- Cornwall and Devon Bear Fairs – organised by Emmary Fairs and held at Exmouth, Devon in May and Lostwithiel, Cornwall in June and November – www.emmarybears.co.uk
- Leeds Doll & Teddy Fair – organised by Dolly Domain Fairs, this event is held in March and October at Pudsey Civic Hall, New Pusdey – www.dolly-domain.com

Museums

- Puppenhausmuseum – glorious museum in Basel, Switzerland which includes some great old Merrythought bears in its wonderful displays – www.puppenhausmuseum.ch
- V&A Museum of Childhood – based in London's Bethnal Green, this off-shoot of the famous V&A houses a vast collection of old toys including teddy bears, a few Merrythoughts amongst them – www.vam.ac.uk/moc
- British Bear Collection – extensive collection of British-made teddy bears, currently on loan to Wookey Hole Caves attraction – www.wookey.co.uk

Publications

- *Collect It* – this glossy monthly magazine addresses all aspects of collecting but includes regular features and occasional supplements on the subject of bear collecting – www.warnersgroup.co.uk
- *UK Teddy Bear Guide* – published annually by Hugglets Publishing, this book is invaluable to collectors as it contains details of fairs, dealers, shops, restorers and much more – www.hugglets.co.uk

Shops selling modern Merrythought bears

- Ironbridge Gorge Museum Shop, Coach Road, Coalbrookdale, Telford, Shropshire TF8 7DQ – www.ironbridge.org.uk/shop
- The Bear Garden, 10 Jeffries Passage, Guildford, Surrey GU1 4AP – www.beargarden.co.uk
- The Bear Huggery, Tower House, Castle Street, Douglas, Isle of Man IM1 2EZ – www.the bearhuggery.co.uk
- The Bear Shops, 18 Elm Hill, Norwich NR3 1HN – www.bearshops.co.uk
- Sue Pearson Dolls & Teddy Bears, 18 Brighton Square, The Lanes, Brighton BN1 1HD – www.suepearson.co.uk
- Teddy Bears of Witney, 99 High Street, Witney, Oxfordshire OX28 6HY – www.teddybears.co.uk

Specialist old bear dealers

- All You Can Bear – specialists in vintage and artist bears – www.allyoucanbear.com
- Bourton Bears – antique and vintage bear specialists – www.bourtonbears.com
- Daniel Agnew – former Christie's teddy bear and soft toy expert, now turned dealer and valuer – www.danielagnew.com
- Leanda Harwood – stocks a large selection of good quality vintage bears and soft toys – telephone 01529 300737
- The Teddy Bear Chest – home to a wide selection of vintage teddy bears dating from 1902 to 1940 – www.theteddybearchest.co.uk

Teddy Bear Restoration

- Dot Bird – specialising in sympathetic restoration of vintage teddy bears – telephone 01765 607131 or visit at Winter BearFest/Teddies Festivals

Acknowledgements

THIS BOOK would not have been possible without the help of a great many people. Oliver Holmes answered my persistent questions about his family history with infinite patience, and John Laxton similarly responded to my requests for information and photos. Former employees Peter Andrews and Jacqueline Revitt spoke freely and with great affection about their days at Merrythought, and Pat Rush was generous with her extensive knowledge and resources relating to the company's history. Merrythought enthusiasts Jill Byron and Angela Popay supplied images, as did expert teddy restorer Dot Bird who also gave me invaluable assistance in the chapter relating to recognising old Merrythought bears. For further images, I am grateful to the unfailing generosity of several specialist old bear dealers including Daniel Agnew, Bourton Bears, Leanda Harwood and All You Can Bear, as well as Lorna Kaufman of Vectis Auctions who never once grumbled when I repeatedly asked her 'for just one more image'. Sue and Malcolm Brewer also helped enormously with images, as did Laura Sinanovitch of the Puppenhausmuseum in Basel and Ian Pout of Teddy Bears of Witney.

For information relating to Clifton Rendle's military record, I am grateful to Mike Motum (RIFLES Secretary) and Richard Kemp of the Somerset Military Museum Trust. I must also give thanks to Barry Edwards at Merrythought, Yuri Shimpo at Archives of Ontario, Michele Pacheco at Sears Canada Inc., and Jan Johnstone whose ability to ferret out useful information is second to none. Finally, my unfailing love and gratitude go to my husband Alastair and daughter Amy who uncomplainingly bore the brunt of my Merrythought obsession.

Further Reading

The Toy Business – A History since 1700 by Kenneth D. Brown

The Magic of Merrythought by John Axe

More Merrythought Magic by Pat Rush

The Teddy Bear Encyclopedia by Pauline Cockrill

Century of Teddy Bears by Leyla Maniera

Picture Credits

Daniel Agnew
Peter Andrews
John Axe
Bourton Bears
Dot Bird
Malcolm Brewer
Jill Byron
Oliver Holmes
Ironbridge Gorge Museum Trust
John Laxton
Tracy Martin
Angela Popay
Puppenhausmuseum, Basel
Jacqueline Revitt
Pat Rush
Sears Canada Inc.
Sarah Sellers
Vectis Auctions

Index